The Ventriloquist

Other Titles by Gary Geddes

Poetry
Poems
Rivers Inlet
Snakeroot
War & Other Measures
The Acid Test
Changes of State
No Easy Exit | Salida difícil
Light of Burning Towers
Girl by the Water
The Perfect Cold Warrior
Active Trading: Selected Poems 1970-1995
Flying Blind
Skaldance
Falsework
Swimming Ginger
What Does A House Want? Selected Poems
The Resumption of Play

Fiction
The Unsettling of the West

Non-Fiction
Letters from Managua: Meditations on Politics & Art
Sailing Home: A Journey through Time, Place & Memory
Kingdom of Ten Thousand Things: An Impossible Journey from Kabul to Chiapas
Drink the Bitter Root: A search for justice and healing in Africa
Medicine Unbundled: A Journey Through the Minefields of Indigenous Health Care

Drama
Les Maudits Anglais

Translation
I Didn't Notice the Mountain Growing Dark

Criticism
Conrad's Later Novels
Out of the Ordinary: Politics, Poetry & Narrative
Bearing Witness

Anthologies
20th-Century Poetry & Poetics
Skookum Wawa: Writings of the Canadian Northwest
Divided We Stand
Chinada: Memoirs of the Gang of Seven
The Art of Short Fiction: An International Anthology
70 Canadian Poets

The Ventriloquist

Poetic Narratives
from the Womb of War

Gary Geddes

Rock's Mills Press
Oakville, Ontario
2022

Published by
Rock's Mills Press
www.rocksmillspress.com

Letter of the Master of Horse was first published in 1973 by Oberon Press.
Copyright © 1973 by Gary Geddes.
War & Other Measures was first published in 1976 by House of Anansi.
Copyright © 1976 by Gary Geddes.
The Terracotta Army was first published in 1985 by Oberon Press.
Copyright © 1985 by Gary Geddes.
Hong Kong Poems was first published in 1987 by Oberon Press.
Copyright © 1987 by Gary Geddes.

For information, including retail, wholesale and bulk orders, contact the publisher
at customer.service@rocksmillspress.com.

Acknowledgements

I owe a debt of gratitude to Dennis Lee and the late Dave Godfrey of House of Anansi for publishing *War & Other Measures* in 1976 and to Anne Hardy and the late Michael Macklem of Oberon Press, original publishers of the other three narrative poems reprinted here. I would also like to thank Per Brask who staged *Hong Kong Poems* at the University of Winnipeg in 1986. Subsequent editions of *The Terracotta Army* were published by Harry Chambers at Peterloo Poets in the U.K. and Susanne Alexander at Goose Lane Editions in Canada, in her lovely but now out-of-print illustrated edition. *Terracotta* was also dramatized and broadcast separately by both CBC and BBC radio and is now being adapted for stage. My lasting gratitude goes to all involved for the moral support of belief, including my long-time friend and Rock's Mills publisher, David Stover.

Contents

War is what happens when language fails.
MARGARET ATWOOD

Letter of the Master of Horse

Cover of the first edition, Oberon Press, 1973

          I was signed
on the King's authority
as master of horse.
Three days
          (I remember
          quite clearly)
three days after we parted.
I did not really believe it,
it seemed so much the unrolling
of an incredible dream.

*

Bright plumes, scarlet tunics,
glint of sunlight on armour.
Fifty of the King's best horses,
strong, high-spirited, rearing
to the blast of trumpets,
galloping
down the long avenida
to the waiting ships.
And me, your gangling brother,
permitted to ride with cavalry.

*

Laughter,
children singing
in the market, women
dancing, throwing flowers,
the whole street covered
with flowers.
In the plaza del sol
a blind beggar kissed my eyes.
I hadn't expected the softness
of his fingers
                moving upon my face.

*

A bad beginning.
The animals knew, hesitated
at the ramps, backed off,
finally had to be blindfolded
and beaten aboard.

Sailors grumbled for days
as if we had brought on board
a cargo of women.

*

But the sea smiled.
Smiled as we passed
through the world's gate,
smiled as we lost our escort
of gulls. I have seen
such smiles on faces of whores
in Barcelona.

*

For months now
an unwelcome guest
in my own body.
I squat by the fire
in a silence broken only
by the tireless grinding
of insects.
I have taken
to drawing your face
in the brown earth
at my feet
                (The ears are
                never quite right).

*

You are waving,
waving. Your

tears are a river
that swells, rushes beside me.

I lie for days
in a sea drier than the desert
of the Moors
but your tears are lost,
sucked
into the parched throat of the sky.

*

I am watched daily.
The ship's carpenter is at work
nearby, within the stockade,
fashioning a harness for me
a wooden collar. He is a fool
who takes no pride in his work,
yet the chips lie about his feet
beautiful as yellow petals.

*

Days melt
in the hot sun, flow
together. An order is given
to jettison the horses,

it sweeps like a breeze
over parched black faces.

*

I am not consulted, though
Ortega comes to me later
when it is over and says:

> God knows, there are men
> I'd have worried less to lose.

*

The sailors are relieved,
fall to it with abandon.
The first horse is blindfolded,
led to the gunwales, and struck
so hard it leaps skyward
in an arc, its great body
etched against the sun.

I remember thinking
how graceless it looked,
out of its element, legs
braced and stiffened
for the plunge.

*

They drink long
draughts, muzzles submerged
to the eyes, set out like spokes
in all directions.
The salt does its work.
First scream, proud head
thrown back, nostrils flared,
flesh tight over teeth
and gums
              (yellow teeth,
              bloody gums).
The spasms, heaving bodies,
turning, turning.
I am the centre
of this churning circumference.
The wretch beside me,
fingers
knotted to the gunwales.

*

They plunge toward
the ship, hooves crashing
on the planked hull.
Soft muzzles ripped
and bleeding on splintered wood
and barnacles.

The ensign's mare
struggles half out of the water
on the backs of two
hapless animals.

*

When the affair ended
the sea was littered with bodies,
smooth bloated carcasses.
Neither pike pole nor ship's
boats could keep them off.
Sailors that never missed
a meal retched violently
in the hot sun. Only
the silent industry of sharks
could give them rest.

*

What is the shape of freedom,
after all? Did I come here
to be devoured by insects, or
maddened by screams in the night?

Ortega, when we found him,
pinned and swinging in his bones,

jawbone pinned and singing
in the wind: God's lieutenant,
more eloquent in death.

*

Sooner or later hope
evaporates, joy itself
is seasonal. The others?
They are Spaniards, no more
and no less, and burn with a lust
that sends them tilting
at the sun itself.
Ortega, listen, the horses,
where are the sun's horses
to pull his chariot from the sea,
end this conspiracy of dark?

The nights are long, the cold
a maggot boarding in my flesh.

*

I hear them moving,
barely perceptible, faint
as the roar of insects.
Gathering,

gathering to thunder
across the hidden valleys
of the sea, crash of hooves
upon my door, hot quick
breath upon my face.

My eyes, he kissed my eyes,
the softness of his fingers
moving. . . .

*

Forgive me, I did not
mean this to be my final
offering. Sometimes the need
to forgive, be forgiven,
makes the heart a pilgrim.
I am no traveller,
my Christopher faceless
with rubbing on the voyage
out, the voyage into exile.

Islanded in our separate
selves, words are
too frail a bridge.

*

I see you in the morning
running to meet me down
the mountainside, your face
transfigured with happiness.
Wait for me, my sister,
where wind rubs bare
the cliff-face, where we rode
to watch the passing ships
at day-break, and saw them
burn golden, from masthead
down to waterline.

*

I will come soon.

War & Other Measures

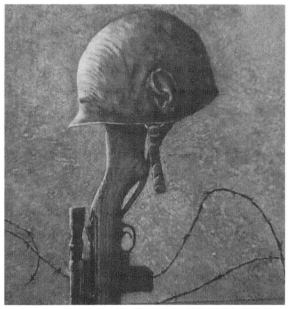

Adapted from the cover of the first edition, House of Anansi, 1976
Watercolour by Roly Fenwick

Book One, Europe 1943

Standing on the escalator
at Piccadilly, she puts her hand
inside my trousers without turning.

Her body on the dirty spread
is covered with scars. She weeps
as I kiss them, her deep wound
closing around me.

I speak of Montreal.
Somehow, my being Canadian
amuses her. Our cigarettes
pencil the darkness.

In the morning she is gone,
the pillow scarred. On the floor
a spent cartridge of lipstick.

*

Train to York in night-time.
Frail child, legs dangling
from carriage seat, her head

an enormous wasps' nest
of bandage. And cradling
a China doll.

Tired man looks up at me,
smiles.

Badly hit, he says. Deaf, too.
Came over high, couldn't
hear until it hit. The whole house.
Doll came through without
a scratch. Fancy that.

*

Travelling by night, stopping in barns
and haystacks (no charge for the rats),
we make it, finally, behind the lines.

Guards at checkpoint, officious,
heel-clicking. Everything in order.
Fournier behind me on a bicycle.

Frightened, wanting only to run.
Walking down the road conspicuous
as a tourist, the back of my neck

grown suddenly bare. Truck stops.
So close, their soft young faces
sucking courage from a cigarette.

Surprised by my own reflection
in the windscreen, five day's growth
and wearing these filthy overalls.

I take the lift they offer.

*

Three sticks of dynamite
well placed under the jeep.
One infantry colonel, one driver,
two ambivalent authorities.

Afterward, the reprisals.
This is war, I say.
                    I have orders.
I have to keep moving, fear
my constant companion.

Wisdom leaking to the winds
like gas.

*

Break the chain of command. Always
the same pattern, a child's game
of checkers: jump one, lose five.

New crop of French widows.

One more grateful than the rest
gives me food and shelter for a week.
As the husband dreams his outrage
in the parlour, I spill my grief
into her body.

Fournier found with a carving knife
in his throat. His smile
infectious, even in death.

*

Talking to myself again,
grown more taciturn than ever
to hide the patois.

My hands fascinate me, two
live animals at my sides.
They feed me, light cigarettes,
help themselves to my things.
Night creatures, they live by day
in my pockets.

I watch them fold and unfold,
move among the objects
on the table, wonder how much
longer they will need me.
I do not want to understand
their language.

*

Fournier's memory always amazed
me, the way he could summon up
physical detail, whole conversations,
and give them a special colouring.

He had been wandering southside
one evening in late October, among
gutted houses, some half standing,
when this kid materializes in a doorway
and says, Penny for the guy mister,
dragging behind him a stuffed pillow-case
tied in the middle and drawn with falling
hairlock and coal-dust moustache.

Bombs intended for Westminster,
dropping short, spending their fury
on the innocent. The kid crouched,
an animal alertness in his limbs,
eyes that could read a face.
Scruffy as hell—and the cheek
of his puppet Führer. Fournier used
the phrase stuffed men of politics
and called the kid one of those
for whom war changes nothing.

I could listen to him for hours.

*

Moon, full and uncooperative,
moving on a grid of cloud.

Running a film of my next move.
In it, I offer the sentry a smoke,
drop it. He does not rise again,
but stretches out in slow motion
among the flowers, head
twisted oddly on its broken stem.

I round the corner of the cottage,
toss two pineapples in the window
and dive for cover.

I miss the sound of his voice
already.

*

running running
somewhere to get to
trees farmhouses dumb cattle
go by me on a painted screen
someone is cranking it backstage
they're shooting again this must be
the second time around

stand of poplars can't get
past it tangled in branches
this is not fair each one
I break grows extra hands

nurse shakes me her full weight
pinning down my arms my eyes

are slow to focus she is smiling
hips draped across the bed
like a pool player's

*

this is a dream i am holding
a small child in my arms the
child's head begins to grow
arms and legs drop away its
features stretch and vanish
it becomes a globe a world
eyes staring from continents
starts to turn in my hands
floats upward past the roof
the treetops I raise my rifle
take aim there is a scream
I am covered in green paint
the doctor will like this one

*

A genuine occasion in the ward.
Two officers shaking my hand,
pinning something on my nightgown.

They smell of authority
and shoe-polish, accents honed
at Oxford and Upper Canada.

My eyes remain closed. I decide
to exploit my role as screwball.
When their ritual is finished,
I release a premeditated fart,
throw the ribbon on the floor.

Everyone is embarrassed.

*

I refuse the doctor's lighter,
(smell of sulphur reaches the nose
first, clings to the membranes)
and begin to talk.

Came home reeking of booze,
face puffed, small pig eyes
receding into his head.
By then she had been gone
six years, and not a letter.
Took a job as night-watchman
at Eddy's, so he wouldn't
be home alone at night.

Wore his best suit to see me off
at the station, then went home
and put a match to the house.
Telegram waiting in London.
Father father, I cried, o jesus,
I loved you.

How deep do these things go,
anyway?

*

Parsons is playing Opus Posthumous
in the lounge again this morning.
Thinks he's poor Schubert
who died penniless at thirty-one.

I pass the window on my walk
and stop to examine a caterpillar,
also unaccompanied, making its way
across the ribwork of a leaf.
It hangs over the edge, swings
its slow body back and forth,
back, and finding nothing,
withdraws its accordion shape.

Music stops. Parsons rises.
Plays well, but never gets past
the Andantino.

*

Funeral services held in my room
at 10:45. I invite the staff
and other patients. There are hymns,
a few prayers, and a brief eulogy
for the departed. The orderlies
wheel it out on a trolley draped

with Harris Tweed, we bury it
in a matchbox. My handkerchief
is wet with smiles.

Doesn't matter what you do,
as long as you do it with style.
I used to think Fournier was queer,
he quoted Oscar Wilde so often.

*

The shrink uses my first name,
lights my cigarette, jokes
about the length people go
to get a few days off.

I tell him again of the Sutherlanders,
trekking overland from Hudson Bay,
about the thick piece of rope
from which Riel dangled.
I want to know about you,
he says, not your country.

My grief is not an ocean
to be crossed, but inside,
black and fathomless.

We both pretend he understands.

*

White sails of the nurses
glide past the open door,
a flotilla of good intentions.
Beamy, deep-keeled girls, more
stable than basic industries.

When the dust settled,
flesh of her breast lay red
and open, dark pool of blood
in the belly's hollow.
A ringed hairy finger twitches
on the hearthrug, then nothing.

Moonlight in the dead eyes
of the sentry.

Book Two, Toronto, years later

Roger stands, motionless, beneath
the hospital trees at the asylum,
999 Queen Street East,
tasting thin shafts of sunlight
with this aide, a Mrs. Altman.
A light breeze troubles the elms,
shadows play upon his face
and arms like motley.

I recall him, just out of school,
stripping an engine in Antoine's garage,
parts everywhere, in hubcaps, newspapers,
wartime headlines covered with grease.
He held up this dirty carburetor
like the torch of Liberty and announced,
proudly, he had joined the Engineers.

A blue Ford passes. He does not identify
make or colour, only the sudden
movement.
                    Hooks of bright chrome
catch in his slow eyes. Briefly, the '37
Ford coupe whisks him away through the silent

streets of his city, past crowds of grey
children waving in slow motion.
Sunday 10 a.m.

*

On the bus downtown
I try to read Mrs. Altman's
thoughts. She has lived,
wept, had her way with men.

Her legs fall apart beneath
the front pages of the *Globe*.
I'm surprised, she says aloud,
an educated man like you.

Forecast for her is bleak:
cloudy, with continuing rain.
A few clear patches on Sunday,
but otherwise no change.

*

We take the October ferry
to Ward's Island.
                    Toronto
floats free, propelled
by unseen feet.

Three ships manoeuvre,
swing their bows
toward the Eastern Gap.

HMCS *Haida* catches the sun
Along its grey length.

My eye moves, rapid-transit
from horizon back to hydro
stacks:
                    bare legs disappear
into the dustbin of commerce,
waxing human and unsuccessful.

*

We're eating at the pavilion.
Roger's large hands dominate
the table, clumsy, grasping,
a Hudson Bay monopoly
on the whole area.

I remember leaving the butter
out. It will melt soon, grow
rancid, black flies
circle it like buzzards.

Roger's face is like the times,
out of joint.

*

Motorized swans glide past
the pavilion door. Mrs A
stretches out on the grass,
starts to unbutton her past.

*My parents, what a pair
of innocents. You should have
seen them.*
              *Words of the prophets
ringing in their ears, saying
the Lord shall comfort Zion,
comfort all her waste places.*

*Scream of prairie wind, saying
build build build until I
stopped up my ears with rags.*

Roger's face at the window
He holds up the quarter tip.
he has taken from the table.

*

Mrs Altman can't be stopped.

*Even the horses were skittish
at his departure. It was crazy.
I mean, married for one year.*

*I hated him for weeks, refused
to write. Something in his eyes,*

an eagerness, as if he had gone
already, body waiting to catch up.

The figures she creates join us
on the boardwalk, with Ward
on his October Island. A uniformed
farmer, pitchfork in hand,
curious unfortunates
with nothing for the sacrifice.

Breath in clouds like speech bubbles:
look up Aunt Edith in Bournemouth

I should have mended that sleeve
Don't forget to write, Harry.

Harry?

*

Three freighters in line
begin the slow crawl seaward.
A million sleeping bushels.

You should have seen me then,
after months in Toronto factories,
stepping from the train, fingers
frozen around the telegram.

Platform was deserted, except
for father. We start seeding

in the morning was all he said,
reins in cracked brown hands.

The ships steam slowly
through the Gap, faintest wash
nudges the retaining wall.

*

I might have known
her husband.
            Ten days
anchored in Bedford Basin,
freezing rain, decks treacherous.
Waiting the birth, the battle
we would all lose.

Ten days. Our thoughts echo
in grey metallic silence.

Downwind, riding,
umbilical.

Bells, rumble of hydraulic
winch, voices over intercom.
This man-child from the prairies
screaming, his fear mirrored
in scrubbed earnest faces.

Leaving it all behind.
Easing into the night swells,
the real
      black
          final
             Atlantic.

*

First night alert. One
of the escort vessels hit
amidships, gone in minutes.
All that is left swept up
neatly along the tide-line.

Oars and bodies intertwined,
lads hanging like puppets
in the strings of preservers.
Recruit from Fredericton,
leaning over the bow, pike-pole
in hand, empties the contents
of his stomach into the blue
faces, oily tresses of kelp.

An empty Huntley-Palmer
biscuit-tin bobs alongside,
red lettering legible, touches
the hull, shatters the morning
like cannon.

*

The munitions factories, as
if the killing would stop, war
surplus widows, thousands
bent in the greater harvest.

Mrs A is not quite finished,
but I'm hooked now. I see her
there, aproned, a Bride of War,
hair done up in a kerchief.

Brass 40mm shells, three
abreast on the conveyor belt
innocent as coke bottles.

*

You have nice legs, he told her,
making his rounds of the shop.
Nice legs, his voice softening
 the roar of machinery…

Those dull eastern days.
His kindness opened her
like a wedge.
                    Stepping down
the St. Lawrence, hardly
any freeboard at all.

Bia River. Halifax City. Poseidon.

League after nautical league
toward the sea, the rush
of locks opening.

*

Where is Roger?

We find him face down
between the motorized swans
in the lagoon, afternoon sun
strafing his swamped blue

body. The seasons have no
respect. Faces of children
sprout from branches, old
men incite the ducks

to anarchy. The swans
are undisturbed, their
stately necks the prows
of Viking ships.

*

Life preservers.
                    Consider
the irony of that term.

Awkward boys, dreaming sun,
dreaming freedom, floating
dead in their waxed water-wings.

Oars cutting the still
surface like a beetle, ship's
sides dissolving in bluish mist.

The way Fournier put it:
only the suck-holes survive.

Book Three, Toronto, 1965

United Brotherhood of Carpenters,
Local 27. Four wedding cars pass,
chauffeur-driven, police escort.
Neo-Nazis haranguing in Allan
Gardens, little demigods
who've never seen the hard
side of bed.
                    This is Peter Martin,
boozer's nose, shiny emaciated face,
but under his frayed shirt-collar
the softest brown skin…

            (I come down from Emerson,
Manitoba. You know, they got salt mines out that way,
own by an Indian guy. I'm just a bum, maybe those guys
up top wanna make trouble, I dunno what they're up to.
Ya, I got a son, I seen him not too long ago maybe ten
year. Big boy, works in the mine. I work high steel, 1100
feet in Chicago, big John Hancock building. Man, that's
a tough kid, cleaned four guys in a bar once in Timmins.
I don't know if he's married. I never ask, don't wanna
bother him.)

He moves off, bear-like,
straight as an arrow, along
his treacherous high beam.

*

I circle the Gardens
twice.
            Mid-winter sun
angles off the mosque-shaped
roof of the glass conservatory.

Pedigreed plants breed
in the controlled climate.

Then west along Gerrard
past the blue-rimmed TV eyes
of derelict houses.

Cut flowers bleed slowly
into pickle jars.

*

I'm in a bar downtown watching
a review of news from the early
sixties body of the president
jerks suddenly like an epileptic
pitches forward in the limousine

the man next to me at the counter

complains about his wife's bladder
problem then, quite unexpectedly
departs to relieve his own

meanwhile, the president spits out
his life I've seen it all before.
this time it's in black and white

his blood is the colour of ink

*

Like that book of Hogarth
in the shop on Yonge Street.

Watching from his
father's shoulders the ritual
of public execution.

Beauty, he says, *is*
a matter of form, a
composed intricacy of form
which leads the eye
and mind a kind of chase.

Thin streams of milk
running down the breasts
of nursing mothers.

*

A toss-up between hockey
(Bruins versus *les Canadiens*)
and some sort of documentary

Above the row of stoppered
bottles, decanted spirits,
Chelsea girls scissor their way
from shop to shop, noting
the latest cut in dresses,
eyeing themselves in windows

Moon ordains their
hemlines as their bodies
must be a CBC special
the obscene lens zooms in
nuzzles the tight posteriors

*

How are these things supposed
to happen, in what order?

I (who was not I) was
here (which was not here)
with another woman
in another year.
                    Moving
among the hustlers, the
news-seller with leprous
nose, tattered violinist
playing Mozart at Charing

Cross, his mate cadging
change from servicemen

*

Sunlight, sleep & waking.
From her vessel the light
pours. The wound in my head.
We've been to see Chaplin
in a film called City Lights.

A fool/saint, pretending
        to be rich for a blind
                flower-girl's sake.

Charlie Charlie, she says,
because of my funny walk.
Her practised fingers arrange
our bodies, pistil and stamen.

Odour of her juices all
day on my hands.

*

It's no good, I can't pretend.

Those dead in the cottage,
pieces all the King's men
couldn't put together.

51

Five senses to remind me,
recall minute details,
how morning light dances
on the row of black helmets.
Steam rising from holes
that blossom in their bodies.

It heals to no more than
a blue scar, an enigma.

*

She imagined her womb an
abandoned warehouse, miles
of umbilicus coiled and hanging

like rotted fire hose. Dreamed
of some last desperate coupling,
begot unnatural creatures that
uncoiled slowly in her
desert places . . .

*

Brown face at the table nearest
me, his body rocking gently in sleep.
Peter Martin, hero and hustler,
Chasing Salvation Army buffalo.

He follows the white arrows
ONE WAY, on green
lamp-posts.

                Next door
at the doll hospital, new heads,
boxes of arms and legs
for the asking.

                That's it, Peter
tells me, to be so easily repaired,
a wooden Indian, to feel,
intensely, nothing.

*

Morrison was at the Brunswick
last night, with his woman as usual.
They occupied the same table
just to the left of the platform.

Meet the little lady, he says.
This is the fifth introduction.

Broken teeth, famed in a thick
swath of orange lipstick. *Nice Piece*,
Morrison says, while she sings
and wiggles her ass on stage,

him clapping, *Nice piece, eh?*
Twenty years in used cars,
Morrison should know better,
bodies become obsolete fast
here in the east, rusted out.
Too much salt in the beer.

*

Learn to use what is there,
create an aesthetic of comedy.

How, at the moment of death,
the bowels discharge.

*

Deaf-mute approaches,
slips his thin white card
into my reluctant hand,
passes to the next table.

Energy that should drive
limbs and voices tumbles
within his sound-proofed
body, as in a penny scale,

delivers this paper tongue.
It's enough. I wear his
presence like a mask.
The four-edged missive

delivers its doleful message
in my skin. A squadron
of print scrambles in
at my eyes.

*

I'm mute, my mind
a slaughterhouse.

Behind these eyes the light
is dying, and the flowers.
Machine-gun night rotates
upon its turret, cuts them
down like infantry.

Charlie Charlie
the voices whisper

where is the blind
flower-girl, who keeps
your image in her fingertips?

*

No roses in this garden
kiss the earth,

they thrust their beauty
skyward, out of reach.

An arsenal of thorns keeps off
the greedy mole,

soft noses of weasels. Silent,
aristocratic,

the tight young buds are
bullet heads.

Book Four, House of Commons, May 18, 1966.

Walking along the canal
toward Parliament a man
standing in bushes opposite,

Tell me about politics,
I shout. You've been here
long enough to see it work.

Every day the minute hand
makes its 24 revolutions,
time's a fiction, its units
collect unemployment insurance.

He glances at me over one
shoulder, replaces himself,
disappears into the shrubbery.

*

This place draws me back
again and again: the manufacture
of destinies, some such perversion.

From its pedestal the column
flutes out like a feather duster
to form 24 perfect arches.

Fossilized limestone interior
from Manitoba, form and content,
the aesthetics of government.

Did Riel ever piss
into that quarry?

*

Caught up in the marble statue
of Victoria in the library.
Her whiteness dominates the room,
oak floor to lanterned dome.

I examine carved door-figures,
beaver and eagle, sad creatures
of establishment. Give me
the solitary blue heron, skimming
the still surface of lagoons.

Victoria stands, bemused
at her captivity. Outside the buttresses
are flying south, to winter

in Washington.

*

I see from the Visitor's Gallery
a Conservative member reading
the *Globe,* Minister of Consumer
Affairs picking his nose.
                    Extension
of the schoolroom. Routine,
rhetoric, debate, the facade
of discussion. Where does the power

reside? My bilingual ears twitch
at theses caricatures of leadership,
performing their obscene dance
along the brink of meaning.

*

It's all a matter
of roots, etymologies.

Dynamite: from the Greek
dynamus, meaning power.

Explode: originally
to drive off stage
by hooting or clapping.

Six sticks. After
twenty years the smell
familiar as skunk.

*

I remember his directions
as if it were yesterday

—Store explosives in cool dry place
—Trim ends of safety fuse, cutting
squarely with clean sharp blade
—Seat fuse gently against explosive
charge in detonator cap
—Keep fuse firmly in place
by crimping
—Plant carefully into dynamite

how the adverbs matter
still in this connection

*

Portraits of prime ministers
down the long corridor.

Maurice, mouth full of sawdust,
sliding down the mountain of chips
at Eddy's. How many matches
in a 30-foot pine, he whispered,
allowing for wastage. M. Poirier
still writing the list of names
(Macdonald Laurier Mackenzie King)
on the blackboard, chalk dust
on the seat of his trousers.

Maurice slumped over the wheel
of his jeep at Dieppe, salt water
lapping his Canadian ankles.

*

a country strung together
hastily, iron and sentiment,
the veneer of civilization

Thompson on a mountaintop
in the Rockies, frightened silly,
charting the northwest territories,
never understanding the contours
of his own mind
                          sits paralyzed
while his voyageurs plod below
in the valley, searching

instruments have not prepared him
for death, at 54 degrees north

Under the skin, the callous,
a man is capable of anything

*

At dockside in Montreal
immigrants stare at me,
wrapped in old nationalities.

I could tell them something
they did not come 4000 miles
to hear. It was there to discover
among their rocks, the billboards.

More than once they must have
felt themselves drifting towards it,
seen trees jump to attention, houses
step quickly into line.

In Toronto, on this knowledge,
they will build an arthritic solitude
in Spadina garment factories.

*

Want something enough
to kill for it.

What does that mean?

D'Arcy McGee bled, learned
nothing from the equation.
And Whelan, his thick neck broken
doing a solo walk in space.

Voices, voices.

We do what we must, according to
voices that speak through us.

*

The doughy substance is worked up
neatly into 1 x 8 inch rolls
and wrapped in waxed brown paper
like stacks of dimes or quarters.

In the fields back of Hull,
showing us the ropes for a little
free labour, old man Mackenzie
ignites the length of black match
and advises –
                "Always use FORCITE
for stumping boys. All you need
is 40%" and laughs, thinking
we didn't get the joke

the dead wood lifting six feet
out of the ground, seeming to hang
there, counterfeit, in the blue
vault of the afternoon

*

I look for Fournier's name
in the Book of Remembrance

Stone lions guard the way
to the Memorial Chamber.
Stained glass windows, altar
of sacrifice. An accommodating god,
always at the service of Caesar

The living dead, thousands
who returned home to jobs, to families
that never noticed the difference

Their souls like butterflies
kept in glass cases. Windows
refuse to bleed, recall
these names, this stain.

*

Now begins the breakup,
the unnaming

that old man on the road
to Perpignan, breathing
through a hole in his throat
hills behind him terraced
to prevent erosion

El senior tiene surgico,
the woman whispers

another kind of language

dry air enters the lungs,
withdraws into the mass
without grammar, syntax

*

my face peers from a window
in the green copper oxide roof,

amazed there is till beauty
in the world, worried
the politicians will find out.

Sunlight strikes the clock-tower,
renders time indistinguishable.
Wrought-iron grillwork casts
strange shadows on the wall
and staircase.
                        Tired of it all,
puns, the poetry of depreciation.

What makes this a necessity
for me and for my people?

*

Battalions of Dutch tulips
occupy the streets, the canal.
Wind from Dow's Lake sweeps

through the columns like a wave.
Reds, delicate yellows strain
to the left on slender stalks.

Faces of deadmen dance, festive,
in the cool May morning, white
toes grubbing the familiar soil.

Spring roots stretch and swell,
thrusting green bayonets
into the pregnant air.

*

Why must there
always be flowers?

The coiled gunpowder fuse
which burns through, leaving
the porous casing hot but intact,
is now called Black Clover.

The sticks refereed to as
DIGEL, a C.I.L. trade name,
70%.

Call it a cottage industry.

Quebec and Ontario chemicals
explode in quiet Asian hamlets

*

One last smoke. It soothes,
gives a shape, an attitude.

Discard the laws of cause
and effect, abolish reason.

There is nothing to be found
beyond the descriptive act.

*

Truth is a snowflake
on the naked eye.

I am a blind man
trying to discern

the shape and texture
of its dissolving.

*

Two facts:

1. I have been intimate
    only with strangers.

2. I have become English, a
    language with no feminine.

If you don't understand this,
blame it on the translation.

*

My face distorted
in the long brass tubing
of the washroom. How it
disappeared that day
as she showered, steam
eating the edges, the
features, condensation
riverring the mirror
like blood.

Turbaned head emerging
from the shower, The child
I could not give her, bandaged,
riding into the darkness
somewhere, on a train.

*

Force of the double explosion
sent the blue lace curtain
billowing out the window,
like a tongue extended.

And Poirot's only daughter,
collaborating with the moon,
the tides, a fragment of grenade
lodged beneath her left ear.

Wartime still-life, heart's wine
leaking onto torn bedclothes.

This is my craft, my art.
Hands go about their business
silent as undertakers.

*

Here is the moment
we've been waiting for.
The vortex. Absolute
zero of porcelain.

I grow smaller.
Shuffle, cap in hand
at the womb's entrance.

*

Cut the throat of the sky,
darkness bleeds into corners
of the evening.

                    In town
a station attendant, one leg
shorter than the other, rides
his body up and down
                        like a pump.

Water lies in pools
along terraces of the mind.

*

I'm raining again
a steady persistent rain

all the truth we know is
scratched on lavatory walls
the masquerade of personality
is over
      the trip to Ottawa
by bus faces in headlights,
engines revving at intersections
a white four-door leading the pack
blur of traffic, the body
of my friend, out of this blood
another rose will burst, its fragrance
confound the universe

*

History is being made,
I am the materials.

The Terracotta Army

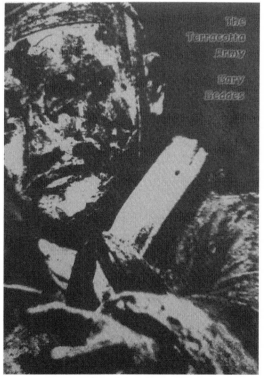

Cover of the first edition, Oberon Press, 1985

Charioteer

So they call you layabouts a standing army?
There's more life in this terracotta nag

than in the whole first division. With that
Bi leapt on the back of a cavalry pony he had fired

the previous day and dug his heels into the outline
of ribs. I wouldn't have been surprised

to see it leap into action and clear the doorway
with the potter shouting death to the enemy.

Most of the animals were cast from a single mould
and could be distinguished one from the other

only by the application of paint and dyes. I took
exception to this and remarked that, as charioteer,

I found more distinctive characteristics in horses
than in men. Bi swung his legs over the neck

and dropped to the ground. He was no taller
than the ponies he fashioned. Then, with a flourish,

he drew a green moustache on the horse's muzzle
and fell about the pottery amused by his own joke.

Spearman

Before double-ninth day, my measure was taken
in a single sitting, so sure were Lao Bi's

eye and hand. The tenth month I returned
with armoured vest and spear and struck a pose

that pleased him so much he laughed out loud
and threw his wineskin at my feet.

He called me the youngest of the Immortals
and promised me a place in the glory-line.

The likeness was uncanny, not just the face,
but the way the sleeves bunched up at the wrists,

studs and fluted leather of the shoulder-pads.
I was drawn to it again and again as if by magic.

One day, without warning, we left for the frontier
and I felt a greater reluctance

to part with this pottery replica of myself
than I had in taking leave of my own village.

Bi used to slap me on the back and say,
you're too serious to be a soldier.

Guardsman

At first I did not like him and put it down
to the arrogance of the creative mind,

his not mine. I'd been the previous day,
guarding the entrance to Ch'in Shi Haung's tomb,

where the artisans and craftsmen were at work
fashioning god knows what final luxuries

for the imperial afterlife. By the sounds of it,
they were feeling no pain. I mentioned this

quite casually, by way of small talk,
to the master potter as he examined my skull

and he exploded like a devil, threatening
to cut off my head for more detailed study.

Needless to say, I wasted no time absenting myself
from his presence and stopped in for a drink

at my quarters. They told me the tomb was finished
and the great door had been dropped into place,

sealing in every artist and workman employed there.
My hands flew, of their own accord, to cover my throat.

Minister of War

I was a young man on the make, a brain for hire,
a travelling politician. I saw my chance,

adopted Ch'in, advised the death of feudal tenure,
not to mention purges and the burning of books.

I scorned the golden mean of men like Mencius
and learned my politics from rats in the latrine;

yet I had respect enough for the written word to know
that old records and systems are better destroyed

than left to seed rebellion and discontent in the period
of transition. The same logic applied to scholars

and authors, those masters of anamnesis, or recall.
I kept the Emperor occupied with toy soldiers

and the arts, or fears of death and court intrigue,
while the real politics unfolded as I knew it would:

highways, taxes, centralization, promotion by exam.
He might have stopped my war against the past,

but I saw to the depths of his and all men's hearts,
where artist lies down, at last, with bureaucrat.

Lieutenant

You might call me a jack-of-all-the-arts;
I paint, draw maps, sing, write a fair poem.

I skipped basic training because of the length
of my tongue and managed to nab a commission

right away in the reserve. I can toss off a lyric
or forge an epic in a single afternoon,

still observing the unities. Once I entered
the Emperor's competition and almost made it

to the finals. As far as visual arts are concerned,
I'm no slouch either. I've been known to sketch

enemy encampments in pitch black, still mounted,
give an accurate impression of slaughter

on the battlefield, avoiding dangerous skirmishes
and ignoring cries for help in order to complete

my precious record. The potter was not impressed.
Learn to write with this, he said, positioning

my hands on the jade hilt of an ornate sword,
the enemy has not yet learned to read.

Paymaster

We stood beside the trenches and looked at the rows
of figures there, bronze horses harnessed in gold

and silver, some of the charioteers in miniature
with robes and hairstyles denoting superior rank;

then the pottery horses with their snaffle bits
and bridles of stone beads. These had been fired

in one piece, except for the tail and forelock.
Most of the men could be seen to wear toques

over their topknots. Kang, of course, had abandoned
such fashions and stood there with an undying leer

and his pot-belly showing through armour, rivets
forever about to pop. A sensualist. I was astounded

as usual by the loving attention to detail and asked Bi
what thoughts this assembled spectacle called up in
him.

Counterfeit currency, he said. A life's work
that will never be seen, poems tossed in bonfires.

A poem lives on in the ear, but a single push
will topple all of these.

Infantryman

We all marvelled at the courage of Ching K'o,
a serious man of letters who loved books

and often drank to excess with dog-butchers
and lute-players in the market-place.

To please the Crown Prince Tan of Yen, who feared
the imminent demise of his kingdom by Ch'in,

Ching K'o agreed to undertake a daring plot
to assassinate the emperor. Delivering the head

of Ch'in's hated enemy General Fan in a box,
Ching K'o unrolled a map of the Yen territories

to be ceded. When the concealed dagger appeared
Ching K'o snatched it up and grabbed the sleeve

of the emperor, but the cloth tore in his hand
and his advantage was lost. Bi laughed

at this turn of events and made some remark
about the advantages of shoddy workmanship.

We tended to ingore his smart-ass comments
and asides, but the irony was not lost on us.

Mess Sergeant

It was not so much the gossip that attracted me
to Bi's pottery, though there was plenty of that:

news of the latest atrocities against the people,
rights and property abolished, heads of children

staring vacantly from terraces, dismembered corpses
turning slowly in the current along the north bank

of the Wei. Rather it was a sort of clearing-house,
a confessional, where our greatest fears were exorcised

piecemeal through the barter of objective detail.
I remember the day when word came of the taking

of Yen. Streets ran with the colour of Ch'in revenge.
The lute-player, Kao-Chien Li, who had plucked Ching K'o

on his way to assassinate the emperor, was blinded
and forced to serenade the victors without ceasing,

blood still running down his face and arms.
Not a sound was heard in the pottery, except the crackle

of logs burning and the sizzle of spit as the last
moisture escaped from the baking clay figures.

Military Historian

And so he standardized everything—axes, measures,
even the language itself. Six of this,

six of that, the uniform evils of power.
What can you say about a man who would burn

books and the keepers of books? So great
was his fear of chaos and the unknown

he was a dupe for any kind of mumbo-jumbo
and excess. One of the wily magicians at court

convinced Ch'in he could find the fabled Island
of Immortals, but must take along the price

not only of gold and silver in great abundance,
but also a host of beautiful youths of both sexes.

Ch'in complied. Nothing more was heard of them.
The emperor put out that they were lost at sea,

but others amongst us presumed the magician
had set himself up nicely on the islands of Fu Sang.

All this came to light much later, when Ch'in
died at the coast, vainly looking out to sea.

Blacksmith

Bi remarked on the lethal aspect of the crossbow,
whose trigger mechanism I'd just improved.

Tests had been done that morning on criminal types
who'd failed to comply with laws on standardization.

At short range the crossbow sent a heavy arrow
through the breasts of five men with surprisingly little

loss of speed. It was equally efficient on two others
in full armour, standing back to back outside the gates

of the A-fang palace. I received a rousing cheer
from the assembled soldiers and nobility;

even the castratos pressed into service in the grounds
and gardens seemed more than slightly impressed.

Bi was sweating profusely and I thought he looked
rather pale in the dim light as he worked on details

of the armoured vest of a kneeling crossbowman.
Where is the Dragon, Rain Bringer, Lord of Waters

when we need him, the potter muttered to himself,
wiping the blade of the chisel on his leather apron.

Harness-Maker

The plot to assassinate Ch'in Shi Huang
was a regular topic at the pottery.

Bi used it as an occasion to sound off about one
or other of his pet theories. What did I tell you,

he said one morning, unwrapping the four bridles
I had just delivered, a man who hangs out

with drunkards and ne'er-do-wells can't be all bad, eh?
No wonder his royal highness never sleeps in the same

bed two nights in a row. And his concubines——
what a waste! How can a man with so much on his mind

keep up his standard of performance? I have it
in strictest confidence from the younger sister

of his current favourite that, contrary to legend,
the Dragon of Ch'in is nothing but a worm

Talk of this sort was confined to a trusted few,
including several peasants who made daily deliveries

of wood and bricks. One, brother of conscript Ch'en She,
squatted like a coiled spring in the corner, grinning.

Strategist

Avoid precipitous cliffs, marshes, quagmires, thickets;
at all times, make the terrain work to your advantage.

Arrive first and lie in wait, rested, fully alert.
Tempt the enemy into the open with shows of weakness.

Don't neglect spies, alliances, the impact of banners, gongs,
drums; detach a flying column, if needed, for a rout.

Better yet, win the war without fighting at all.
Information's the thing. What weapon or scaling-device

can replace the trained ear? Nothing, at least
not in my books. There is no sure defence against a good

pair of eyes. The Five Factors remain constant,
and the Five-Year Plans, but what are economies of war

when increased levies exhaust a people's substance
and spirit and bring the aggressor to his knees

before the enemy? Remember, prolonged war is folly;
so, too, is laying siege to a walled city.

Without these principles the whole empire, not just
the imperial army, will be in ruins.

Spy

I'd read Sun Tzu,
that was my mistake,

read his Art of War
and committed it to memory.

Li Ssu was impressed; otherwise,
he might have left me alone

tending what few books remained
in the imperial library.

I was without status, no beauty either,
nondescript, down at the heels,

nobody's idea of a good time.
But I had my uses.

I was designated Category Five,
the surviving spy,

and ambled freely between the court
and Bi's establishment,

letting my body go to pot
but not my cover.

Commando

My youngest brother disappeared without a trace
after the first recruitment. He was a musician

of no small promise, had anyone bothered to inquire,
and might have piped the hearts of simple men

to victory or wrapped their deadly wounds in notes
of purest silk. Did he lend his flesh to the rubble

of a wall or make his bones instruments of war?
Don't ask. The new carts rattled by on their standard

axles, half-empty. Next they bred a line of faceless
conscripts. Forced labour and conscription

destroyed the base of agriculture, brought revolt.
Who's to say it wasn't for the best?

You can tell by the lightness of my armour
I'm a crack trooper, trained to take the initiative

in battle. I prayed daily my strength would win
sufficient honours to bring me into the presence

of Ch'in and his bloody Councillor, to strike
a chord that's truly worthy of my brother.

Unarmed Footsoldier

Education does not win battles or put bread
on the table. I was a student once, I know.

I had my champions, my favourite causes;
afternoons I was not gallivanting in full heat,

I spent debating the meaning of the universe.
Why did I bother? There's nothing quite like war

to clear the head——or remove it. I was drafted,
I became the perfect machine, precision tool

for the mechanics of death. I was programmed
to kill. I did not need spear or crossbow:

a well placed blow would kill an ox or man
instantly; my special kick was called

the eunuch-maker. Still, my previous studies
were not entirely in vain. I was able to apply

the psychology I'd learned to outwitting the enemy
and, of course, my rivals within the ranks.

The potter read my story to the letter:
poised, unbalanced, deadly hollow.

Captain of the Guard

Is there no aesthetic consistency anymore,
that's what I want to know.

I registered a complaint, after the first sitting,
that he had taken more time braiding the tail

of a cavalry pony and stippling the sandals
of a kneeling warrior than he had taken

getting the fine detail of this face, which
has turned more than pottery heads in its time.

The next thing I know he's placed the head
of that ugly recruit, now bearded, on the six-foot

frame of an officer and recorded for posterity
my untrimmed growth of whiskers.

No, I don't think it was the booze, at least
not primarily. A man like that creates

his own demons and opiates. Realist or formalist—
choose your poison. Was Ch'in drunk

when he shaved a mountain that thwarted him
and had it painted red, as a warning to all nature?

Unit Commander

I was never too keen about the shape of my ears,
the way they hang there like two horseshoes

someone had stuck on as an afterthought.
So I can't say I was anxious to be duplicated

by this barbarous Southerner, whose words fell
about my feet like shards, kiln-dried and jagged.

We talked at length about Ch'in's appropriations,
not just the women, art and slaves

acquired from the defeated princes, but also designs
of palaces and gardens ordered to be copied

and reproduced in Hsienyang, as if a man
might live in more than one house at a time.

He raged against the slipperiness of Immortals,
even immortal rats in their underground mazes;

then he went on, too long according to my notes,
about lack of imagination among peoples of the north,

how even into death they must carry a representation
of the living world. I couldn't believe my ears.

Quartermaster

Seize reality in the act,
embrace its opposites like a lover,

without moderation. That's the ticket.
Though the flesh be captive,

insurgent thoughts invade the palace grounds,
storm the reviewing-stand. Freedom is born

in the anarchy of spilled blood.
Did I say that, or was it Master Bi?

He spoke so close to my ear as he applied
clay to mould my features that his ideas

invaded my brain as if I were a puppet.
Certainly I don't remember propositions

of that sort ever troubling my professional self,
whose sole task was the dispensing of goods,

not words: weapons, food, clothing, rivets, lumber,
and sundry items for the conduct of war.

And no-one ever came to my tent and said:
Hey, buddy, give me a new idea, size five and a half.

Archer

He told me the Emperor's eunuch had paid a visit,
then Ch'in Shi Huang himself, disguised

as a standard-bearer. I was half-mad with curiosity
to know what transpired between them. Instead,

I made some joke about the Great Ch'in
apprenticing to a potter. Bi mimed the action

of the crossbow and told me I was on target
as usual. Damn it, he shouted,

the man is hedging his imperial bets!
He knows he'll be judged by the company he keeps,

even underground. I told him I had neither power
nor inclination to fashion a god, simple as that.

Never mind, it's done. He's given me a month
to reconsider, while he swims and scans the seas

for some immortal vessel. Here Bi took my hand
in his terrible grip as if it had been an injured

bird. I felt his breath on my face as he spoke:
A man must know where his destiny lies, eh?

Lookout

For days he could not be found and was rumoured
to have returned to his boyhood home near Guilin,

where he had been a fisherman. Others claimed
he was sleeping off a drunk. Nothing was mentioned,

but his hand seemed less steady and his eyes
had a faraway look. Don't consider it odd if I dwell

overlong on your face, he said, it is perhaps my last
and will accompany me to the land of the White Snake.

He asked if I believed in astrology and practised
the lively arts. I told him I was a simple lookout

who could spot signs of movement a long way off
and keep a warning beacon alive in all kinds of weather

but, beyond that, I had no theories or opinions.
It occurred to me he might be a bit deranged,

what with working near all that heat and fumes.
Then he told me things about myself that scared me

and some that sent me back thinking I wasn't such a bad
chap, after all. You can't fault a man for that.

Regimental Drummer

He refused, of course, to acknowledge the likeness
and huffed a good deal when I mentioned it.

I supposed he had a cousin in the imperial guard
but recalled a conversation weeks before

when he'd claimed to have no living relatives.
This is my family now, he'd added, pointing

to several terracotta figures in the corner.
But there wasn't the slightest doubt;

this unarmed soldier, turned slightly to reduce
the target area, legs apart, hands ready to parry

or strike a blow, was none other than Bi himself.
Portrait of the artist as master of martial arts,

in the front line, ready for anything, even his warts
rescued from oblivion. We drank a lot of wine

that night and danced around the pottery, reciting
poems and beating drums for the unsung dead.

A slight smile played around the lips and I found myself
winking at the copy instead of the original.

General

If this is what we have evolved toward,
I have to laugh. The illusion of full knowledge

gave us a sinister edge. We became the crassest
of materialists and would tolerate neither doubt

nor disturbing hypothesis. In a word, vulgar.
How easily the innocent joy of the enthusiast

gives way to the intolerance of the true believer.
We began, like all the others, with a vision:

unification, call it what you will. The sorcery
of a fixed idea. For this we marched long years,

long miles, until, winning the war, we found we had
lost face. We became the new reactionaries,

eliminating, in short order, all the best minds.
Not everything is dangerous to the body politic.

Being the son of a farmer, I should have remembered
that certain organisms must not only be allowed,

but also actively cultivated. Nature can be studied,
but never controlled or predicted with absolute precision.

Minister of War

It's not because of superior rank or position
I'm allotted extra space to speak.

I merely have twice as much to answer for.
I was the right hand of God, responsible

for carrying out the wishes of the Leader.
I grew to be more than a soldier——or less.

A politician, which the potter describes cleverly
as a freak of nature that soars above the crowd

but still has ears close to the ground. Of course
I admired Master Bi. We were inextricably linked

by our humour and intelligence. He spoke in riddles
to confound the wise, but also to spread unrest

among the rank and file. I had plans, my own art
to pursue. I exercised decorum,

arranged for another artist to betray him.
Records were kept, tongues loosed

in the usual ways. The plot, discovered,
required a dénouement.

Chaplain

Someone will break us of the habit of war
by taking away our weapons

and we will march against the darkness
(or will it be light?) naked as new-born babes,

tiny fists opening and closing on nothing.
The only certainty, even under the earth, is change,

whether it be cosmetic, paint flaking away
down the muted centuries or

something more violent that destroys the form
itself, icons of public and private selves.

With such thoughts I addressed the potter
on more than one occasion, thinking to shock him.

I'd given up the Tao and had even less time
for the ethics of Confucius in the new dispensation.

Rituals and ancestor worship are as useless to soldiers
as scapulimancy and tortoise-shell prophecy.

Only our vanity is monumental, the potter said,
and that, too, can be broken.

Standard Bearer

Who remembers names or issues now?
The wall that taxed us to the limits

stopped neither time nor barbarians.
Birds flew freely over the battlements,

testing the currents of non-aligned air;
so, too, did the arrows of our adversaries.

Then the enemy himself learned to fly
by subtle propaganda into our hearts

or by invention into our very midst,
wreaking havoc like a berserker.

I joined the potter in his rest;
I broke his ranks but could not break his will.

Only our forms endure. And stubborn words
which hover and adhere, attend our passing

like faithful retainers. Remnants
of an age when the mind groped its way

in darkness, without maps of logic or conquest,
sweeping in its wake the relentless dust.

Hong Kong Poems

From the cover of the first edition, Oberon Press, 1987

1

Rising sun

is a habit of mind
appearing over the edge
of the Atlantic each morning
to the weary garrison,
raw Township boys
and hoary vets of the last war
with no use for astrology

is nuclear fission, constant emission
of heat, light & radioactivity

is symbol painted on steel plates
just above the waterline of a passenger ship
in Manila Harbour, bull's eye
to Johnny Canuck
en route to Hong Kong

is eight minutes ahead of itself,
given the distance and speed
of light

is a flag in a shop window
in Wanchai, looking like a huge fried egg
to passing POWs,
the last egg they'll see
for 3½ years

KRAVINCHUK

We're out back
of the reservoir
when this Nip plane
comes over the ridge
and opens fire.
As the shells hit
a trail of dust devils
snakes toward us
across the valley.
We stand gaping
like a couple of yokels
until it's just about
overhead, then dive
into the makeshift bunker.
Harris starts screaming
I'm hit, I'm hit,
O god, Sam, you can
feel the warm blood
on my shoulder.
His tragic look
is so authentic
you'd think
he'd rehearsed it
from old movies.
He'd have run off
screaming like that, too,
if I hadn't grabbed
both his ankles
and shouted:

Tea, you stupid fucker,
tea. I spilled the thermos
down your back.

GYSELMAN

Among the documents
you'll find a picture of me
standing on a railway tie
at the Winnipeg station,
a cigarette in my fingers.

The puff of smoke I exhale
looks like Scotch thistle
on my tunic lapel.
My face has the arrogant leer
of an evangelist.

Two months later
a quarter of us would be wounded
or dead and I'd dream nightly
of rats
eating dead Japanese.

2

The *Awatea* and *Prince Rupert* have just set sail from Vancouver Harbour. Of course, the expression "set sail" is an anachronism in the age of steel turbines, but no-one is thinking about such fine discriminations of language as the ships swing into First Narrows and head toward the Lions Gate Bridge.

Irene has driven to the docks to watch the ships and now she is driving past Lost Lagoon in a small blue coupé with her father and two sons, one seven years old and reading a book in the back seat, the other sixteen months and standing in her lap twisting her nose and lips. Offers have been increasing since she won the contest as Miss Wrigley Spearmint Gum, but this is her day off work as a demonstrator at Eaton's and she's determined to enjoy herself.

"Mummy, where are the ships going?"

"Nobody knows." Earnest face turned up from its book. Enough to break your heart.

"Well, how will the captain know which way to steer?"

The captain, a good question. Was he the officer who winked from the gangplank? Handsome men in their tight blue uniforms. The decks awash with soldiers, waving, whistling. The tune the band struck up was "Good Night, Irene." And the women? More than just grief in their faces. At least Ann and I have our men safely at home.

Topside, there's a soldier leaning against the gun-mount of the quarterdeck. Pain has begun in his lower abdomen he will dismiss as seasickness. As it worsens, he'll seek medical help but be accused of malingering. Dying, he'll hear waves pound against the hull and steady, rhythmic beat of the engines.

Several officers of C Force are in the mess discussing the missing transport vehicles and the mutton mutiny of the previous day, when soldiers tried to disembark to protest against the cramped quarters and greasy fare. A massive court martial is dismissed as too disruptive to morale. The YMCA officer sits apart, thinking of his wife and Homer's verses on the Trojan horse, while the ship carves its lethal way through through the waters of Burrard Inlet.

The coupé has reached the end of the parkway now and moved onto the bridge, just as the bow of the *Awatea* comes abreast of the span.

"Did Daddy and Grandpa build those ships?"

She looks at her father, the other Grandpa, pipe in his teeth, conscious of the immense bulk passing below. Even above the smoke, she smells the grain on him, a smell that engulfed her childhood, her entire life. Trips back and forth to small farms on Lulu Island, then to the docks. Buckerfield Seeds.

"Mother, will the ships sail away over the horizon?" The cowlick above his high forehead wobbles.

"Yes, dear, perhaps as far as China. Tonight, we'll look at the atlas and make up a story about it." Don't let anything escape you, Renee, this is your day off: pipe smoke, salt air, grain, ripe diapers.

"Will they all die, Grandpa? Uncle too?"

"What's this nonsense?" Words divide around the clenched pipe-stem, re-form."Of course they won't all die."

DALZELL

Tried selling in Toronto
but never made a dime.
Took off on freights
with eight other guys
for North Bay,
but the bulls kicked us out.
Had to work on a road gang
in Capriol for rations.
Got organized in '33
with a soup-kitchen on Water Street,
two meals a day.
Harvested a while,
worked as a cook at Shilo.
After the march to Ottawa
the camps were broken up.
Did sweat work for CPR
at Kenora in '35,
bought an Indian's tent
and camped out.
Married a widow with kids
in 1936 in Winnipeg.
Worked in lumber yards,
cleaned streets for 20 cents
an hour plus meals.
Rent was $14 a month.
That's why I joined up.

MCCRAE

Hell, we had none of that Depression crap.
Us boys were in a spending mood
and, by god, we'd transform Hong Kong's economy
overnight, changing dollars into wine,
feeding the four million Chinese
(or was it two then?).
No cheapskates in D Company,
not like the bloody Limeys.
Workers, blokes who never had two-pence
back home in Leeds or Manchester,
hired Chinese coolies for a dime
to make beds, wash socks,
and rode through the streets
in rickshaws like the King.
It made you want to puke.
So you can understand
why we chose the Sun Sun Café,
which the Brits never patronized,
just a few Rajputs and Punjabis.
We were in high gear, knocking them back
and singing "Roll Me Over in the Clover,"
So no-one noticed the English NCOs
come in and start hustling the girls.
Suddenly this overweight Limey
insults the beaver. I could hear
muscles tighten in a hundred backs.
His mate tries to stifle him,
but someone at the next table
picks up the refrain

and goes on about colonials
being beaver-fuckers
and not knowing one end from the other,
which is why they're all under-endowed.
When the last Limey dragged himself outside,
we threw the Wurlitzer down the stairs
after him, still playing.
The proprietor never said a word.
He was standing on the bar
cheering us on. The guy
had relatives in Vancouver
with apartments on Commercial Drive,
so we were A-okay. By god
if the Japs had attacked that night
instead of the next morning,
we'd have driven them back up the ass
of Colonel Tanaka. Nobody
insults the beaver.

WARNING TO LITERARY FIFTH COLUMNISTS

What I'm doing here is not writing,
but rewriting; and you're neither listening
nor reading, but quietly deconstructing this poem
I've worked so bloody hard on. Harold Bloom
calls it "aftering" or "creative misreading,"
fancy words for plain theft.
You're not the least bit interested
in how I think or feel or express myself;
what you want to know is how to eliminate me
and my words and replace them with your own version
of things, escape your fallen self
and take revenge of time. Well, watch out.
I didn't read *Poetry and Repression*
just for fun. Because I know your plans
and because I have no intention of being supplanted
by you or your rival text, I've mined this poem
with booby-hatches, trapdoors, pitfalls
and anti-reduction devices. Twenty crossbows
are set to fire when the main door opens.
This poem should give you such anxiety of influence
you'll want to gather and burn every copy
as a petty triumph over the inimitable.
That avenue's covered too;
you might as well go home and run a bath.
There'll be no iconoclasm today, no breaking
of the vessels. You can catalogue compulsively,
scribble psyches, and remake archetypes, even try
defensive irony as a means of aesthetic limitation;

but it won't work. This text is armed to the teeth
against all eventualities; free leave has been cancelled
and all eyes are fixed on the shifting horizon.
We'll fight until the tropes come home.
What, you ask, does Harold Bloom say
about subversion from within the poem itself?
Harold who?

3

Close-up of soldiers on duty
in 1941 at Shamshuipo Camp.
They pose on steps, one at ease,

one at attention, two kneeling,
and grin for the photographer
who might have been a friend.

Knapsacks over chests, rifles diagonal
from right hip to left shoulder.
One remembers the stranger

in the men's room at Regina,
who gave him fifty dollars, a uniform
and a new identity, then went AWOL

out of the train station, wearing
striped overalls and boots with no socks.
One anticipates a rendezvous later

at the Sun Sun Café in Wanchai:
red silk dress and almond skin.
One forgot to polish his boots

and hopes the duty officer won't notice.
One has nothing in his head
that might be called a thought,

yet he too smiles. Four Canadians
on duty. What you notice first
is the length of the bayonets.

HENDERSON

I did most of my fighting in Repulse Bay
in a hotel half-full of civilians.
We took up position in a plush suite
on the second floor.

One of the men sat in an armchair
scanning hills out back with binoculars.
When he spotted movements, I'd swing
into the window and fire, then drop back.

Suddenly there was a woman in the doorway
saying, My dog, I'm looking for water for my dog,
We pulled her down out of the line of fire
and gave the dog radiator water we used for tea.

Later, when the Japanese were two football fields away
and their planes were dive-bombing the barracks,
I thought of that woman and her parting comment:
If he bothers you by barking, shoot him.

SULLIVAN

There's a strange hush at St. Stephen's
as we wait for them to storm the College.
Nurses drift like butterflies among the injured,
offering a word, a touch, a cigarette.
when the enemy bursts through the door

I'm lying on a cot at the far end of the corridor,
my head bandaged, my leg supported in a sling.
Two soldiers proceed to bayonet the sick and wounded
in their beds, to a chorus of screams and protests.
A nurse throws herself of top of one of our boys

to protect him—it might have been the kid
from Queen's—and they both are killed
by a single thrust of the bayonet.
I suppose they were sweethearts. Pinned
at last, she does not struggle. Her hands

open and close once, like tiny wings,
and the dark stain on her white, starched uniform
spreads like a chrysanthemum, a blood-red sun.
I cut the cord supporting my leg, slip on
the nearest smock and stand foolishly at attention,
making the salute. My right index finger
brushes the damp cotton of the bandage.

Later, the butchers are shot by their own officers;
one, apparently, had lost a brother
in the final assault.

CURRY

I recall a rice paddy back of Kowloon,
a temple set in the middle.
Mountains in the background are faded,
but more advanced rice stands out
in rows above the water.

Overturned wicker baskets
are used as tables to display produce.
When they don't contain bok choi
or onions, they display the small
round face of a child.

4

I spent several mornings in the office of the *South China Morning Post,* reading copies of *Hong Kong News,* produced after the Japanese victory on Christmas Day in 1941. Early sun glinted off the high-rises and office towers in Victoria as I crossed on the Star Ferry and a huge Bayer Aspirin sign on the roof of a building confirmed my impression of the Crown Colony as a colossal headache.

I was staying in an unheated room in Chungking Mansions on Nathan Road, Kowloon-side, a high-rise slum that offered a rich assortment of internationals selling silk, sex and semi-precious gems. Ascending in the creaking elevator, you witnessed a discontinuous film-strip of erotic tableaux, heated arguments and half-finished transactions.

The cluster of rooms on the seventh floor was bucolic by contrast and had an air of exhausted camaraderie that surprised me, a tribute to the two families of Chinese who ran the place. My room looked out on a alley, a dark, awesome abyss that separated me from the balconies and opulent suites of the Holiday Inn. For only four dollars a night, I could switch my lights lights off and, unobserved from my window, watch the comings and goings in those expensive rooms. Or I could gaze at the stars through a cloud-cover of laundry hanging out to dry on the floor above.

I soon tired of both astrology and low-grade voyeurism and made the rounds of the local bars, particularly the Ship's Inn, run by a Vietnam veteran who'd parlayed his injuries and discharge into a small fortune on the black market. He'd also developed certain tastes that only the Orient could satisfy.

Jim was curious about my mission in Hong Kong, gathering information about Canadians killed or incarcerated there during the war. He ventured it was only non-combatants who wrote about the war. I nursed my glass of bitters and thought of Wilfred Owen, Charles Yale Harrison, even the Royal Rifles' own William Allister. Jim's stitch-marks ran from one ear down across his throat to the other shoulder, like a tiny rope ladder on a helicopter. I said I supposed he was probably right.

5
SONG OF THE BARBED WIRE

I make my first appearance in this legend
east of Wainwright, along the Fifth Concession,
stretched between poplar poles, staples
pounded in to keep me taut.

I was taught all right, taught to do a job—
containment—so I practised on buffaloes,
then on German POWs, lucky if they'd known,
cooped and insolent in tropical gear
near Kingston Town.

I graduated with Honours, trotted out
my scrolls for public scrutiny.

Untroubled by loyalty or scruples,
I served both sides at once: those boys
who jeered their inmates in the tropics
now are jailed themselves, their shaggy mains
not worth a Yankee nickel in this caper.

A little culture rubs off on me, a little flesh,
sins of commission, small retainer fees.
I turn up at the trials in Tokyo drunk,
unstrung, offering to keep the sun in check.

I know my first concession
will be may last.

JOKE FOR THE DAY

INTERNMENT is a great social leveller.
Peakites and Kowloonites are now rubbing shoulders.

PROULX

I was a stockbroker and amateur jockey,
so I spent a lot of time at Happy Valley
and the Club. Ottawa was a long way off.

I knew the market price of commodities
like trust. Hong Kong was down the drain.
So that's how we went too, right out

the storm sewers to a waiting vessel.
Marsman and I escaped and both wrote books
about it. Others were not so lucky.

Three men captured were imprisoned 21 days,
made to dig their own graves, then shot.
Payne, Berzenski, Adam and Ellis

were caught boarding a sampan, interrogated
by Inouye, beaten and promptly shot.
Three hundred Hong Kong dollars

could not keep us afloat on that market
and we had to swim
the last three miles to China.

ANDERSON

One of the jobs I had
after emigrating from Sweden
was in the freezer department
at Swift's, shipping
cheap meat and bacon to Japan.

Military life was good.
When the Pats discharged me
as an alien, I signed up
with the Grenadiers and said
I was born in Alberta.

There's hardly a thing
the Chinese didn't invent.
You name it: noodles, paper,
printing, the compass,
even gunpowder, yet
they had to step off sidewalks
to let the British pass,
then the Japanese.

Major Boone shaved his head
and bowed to the rising sun.

HARDY

I belonged to the millionaires' club.
You know, guys like Ross and Clarke
from Montreal. One of them owned
Great Lakes Steamships; the other
flew his own cook to Hong Kong
and put him up in a Kowloon hotel.

Me, I was eating a cheese sandwich
on my lunch hour from Eaton's
when I saw the recruiting banners.
This sergeant buttonholes me and says:
Join the Grenadiers and winter in Jamaica.
What the hell, I thought, why not?

I cycled over to Main Street,
was driven to the Minto Armouries
and given a uniform.
Mother couldn't believe it;
neither could I.

Such a big-time spender, I left my bike
against a lamppost in the street.
I went back to Eaton's after the war.
Why did it happen? Don't ask me,
that's not my department.

6

The prime minister knew what Churchill said
concerning the defence of Hong Kong.
He wrote the words more or less verbatim
In his diary:

> Let us devote ourselves to what is possible.
> Japan will take Hong Kong, beyond the shadow
> of a doubt, when the time comes. Think
> only of a presence.

Symbolic garrison, that was
the operative phrase.

But he knew, also, the words
of a mother in Moose Jaw
who would not release the hand
he extended until he heard
her thoughts about war:
a farm dying from neglect
while husband and son
rot in the Yorkshire rain.

He did not bother to tell her
they were among the ranks
that booed his presence
in their midst in England.

He saw blood. Privately,
of course. And it was blood

he knew would bring them round
to the war effort.
The blood of mothers' sons
spilled on foreign soil.
So he gave the nod to Crerar
and prayed forgiveness
from his dearest Mum.

DISTINGUISHED SERVICE DECORATIONS

Pellagra
is a vitamin-deficiency disease
that produces sores on the skin,
red and weeping sores, as well as ulcers
on the lips, gums, tongue and throat.

It also has a tendency to cause
severe irritation and chafing
around the genitals. Thus
the nickname: Rice Balls
and Strawberry Balls.

The three Ds of pellagra are
Dermititus, diarrhoea, dementia.

BOWEN ROAD HOSPITAL

I've seen temporary loss of memory in lads
after a raid. Simple inhibitory response
of the brain to excessive stress.
Sleep reduces intellectual activity,
letting the brain and nervous system rest.
Withhold sleep for an extended period,
or interrupt it, and you break down
the inhibitory factors. Drugs
might have worked well enough
if we'd had any to administer.
He seems to have lost consciousness
after the Japanese bayoneted him
and pushed him down an embankment.
Who's to say he was lucky?
He turned at the last moment
and deflected the blow as it grazed
one rib and then made a real mess
of the muscles and bone in the upper arm.
We had to take it off just below
the shoulder. He awakened at night
to the sound of shells exploding everywhere.
He was already weak from loss of blood
and could barely extricate himself
from under the weight of a dead comrade,
let alone crawl toward safety, wherever
that might be. When they brought him in
he was in shock. Bomb happy, they call it.
Aural stimuli, such as grenades and bombs
had caused reflex inhibitions in other areas,

so he had this fixation on getting out
and rejoining his company, at any cost,
with no thought for the deplorable state
he was in. When we ran out of gin,
he had to be restrained. Unfortunately
this fixed state of excitation gave way
to a pathological level of inertia
that would have been more or less permanent,
if blood-poisoning hadn't taken him first.

BERTULLI

It was a carry-over
from the class system back home.

The officers never overcame
their elitist training;
not even imprisonment
could make us equal.

Take the MO, for instance.

An excellent doctor in the field,
but after the war, as far as I
could figure, he sold us out
for a cushy government job.
He was a chocolate soldier,
a fraternity boy who took courses
to qualify as major.

Nobody knew our medical histories
better than he did: blindness,
heart failure, mental breakdown,
suicide. But where was his voice
in the debate for compensation,

hundred per cent pensions?

VARLEY

We were an odd lot, with Orville Kay
a crown attorney, as CO
and under him petty criminals
he had sent to Stony Mountain,
crime-sheets long as your arm.

They lacked nothing in courage
and were as devoted to Crawford
as anyone in sick-bay, myself
included. The Commandant
used to lecture us and blamed all
deaths on the orderlies
and medical personnel.
One day he beat Crawford badly
about the head and shoulders
and threatened to behead anyone
who claimed to be doing his best.

I don't know what came over me,
but I found myself stepping forward,
shaking Crawford's hand, and
following the sergeant out back.

The Commandant was impressed
and things eased off after that,

for a time.

CRAWFORD

I started with a billiard table
for operations. No supplies,
no drugs. Everywhere you looked
men were making apparatus.
Wilcox found a damaged straight razor
and spent two days removing the gouge
with a stone. It was all ad hoc.
An eye-chart to do visual acuities,
with Chinese ink on white paper;
and a dingus to measure peripheral vision.
Then they made an adjustable table
and an ingenious peanut-oil lamp:
reflectors concentrated the light.
The Japanese idea of health care
was to send us gallons of Lysol:
keep camp clean, no disease.
Quarantine for dysentery was one strand
of barbed wire; diphtheria, two.
Selwyn Clark managed to smuggle in
some Thiamin, in a Prayer Book
with help from interpreter Watanabi,
so we had a little Vitamin B
for the worst cases of beriberi.
Some men kept their feet on tiles
or out of windows to cool them.
Others used to soak their feet
for relief; however, this softened
or mascerated the skin, so infection
could set in, then gangrene.

It meant patrolling
the latrines.

7

—Sir, I can't go.

—I know, Jim, you're too sick. I'll send Al.

—You can't do that, Sir. He's worse off than I am.

—I have to send someone.

—I'll go.

MALLORY

Work party again at 6 AM. Low-lying fog over the harbour as we board the ferry that takes us from Shamshuipo to Kai Tak. Bitter cold. Can see only the Peak over Victoria now. No wonder money builds high up, a hedge against fire, flood, disease, the poor.

I'm working alongside Delisle, who can barely raise his shovel, never mind singing in his perfect tenor voice. The poor devil has been down in sick-bay for weeks with dysentery and electric feet. The grey skin is stretched over his bones like kite paper. I try to cover for him by working a little faster than usual, but I know I can't keep up the pace. There must be a hundred of us working on the Reclamation, dumping earth from the high ground to extend the runway into the sea. You have to keep moving or freeze.

"Dumby, speedo!" The guards are shouting to our left, trying to make better time. I suppose they get more rations if the work goes well and a few extra inches are gained each day.

I fill Delisle's baskets as lightly as I can and help him up with them, He moves off ahead of me, so thin he looks as if he might crumble under the weight. The concentration required to put one foot ahead of the other must be enormous, but he plods toward the fabricated shoreline. He's not quite over the dysentery and the backs of this legs are stained from the thin bile that passes through him. He resembles a mechanical scale, the two baskets suspended from the ends of a pole at slightly different levels at his sides.

If we can make it to the edge without attracting attention, no-one will notice the size of his load. We are only twenty yards from the water when one basket dips below knee-level and brushes the ground. It's just enough to betray him. He falls straight forward on his face. The wicker baskets, unfortunately, remain upright and reproachful beside him.

I stand at attention, my legs aching under the weight. Delisle does not move, I think his heart has given out, but I can hear him whisper.

"Je m'excuse, Alvin. Je m'excuse."

Two guards are kicking and shouting. They drag him onto his feet and knock him back and forth between them like a rag doll. One of them reaches into a half-filled basket and throws a handful of dirt into his face. The closed eyes seem to infuriate him as much as the baskets.

"Dumby, cheat. No good."

Delisle's bowels choose that moment to discharge, though he has eaten nothing for days. It's a miracle of creation, or of critical acumen. The guard's face contorts and he strikes Delisle in the mouth with his rifle butt. Then they are dragging him to the water's edge. All work on the Reclamation has stopped. He is on his knees and has begun to sing one of those folksongs that have followed us from Sherbrooke to Newfoundland across Canada and aboard the *Awatea*. I can feel my legs giving out and the bamboo pole cutting into my shoulders. The fog is breaking up and sunlight reflects off the sword as it falls, repeatedly, on his neck. He's remained somehow on his knees and has to be pushed over. One of them kicks his head down the small embankment into the sea.

Several of us are detailed to dig a shallow grave and he is buried, headless, beneath the runway of the Kai Tak airport.

8

The Department of National Defence regrets that it cannot release medical documents, on the grounds that their contents might prove an embarrassment to the men and their families.

HONG KONG NEWS

There are male and female dragons
and they are different.

The male has rough, jagged horns,
deep eyes, wide nostrils, a pointed mane
and thickly growing scales.

The female has wavy-surfaced horns,
a flat nose, a smooth mane,
round eyes and thin scales.

While the strength of the male dragon
is in the upper part of the body,
the tail is the strongest part
of the female dragon.

9

By the end of the first week, I'd made the rounds of all the well known battle sites, including Gin Drinker's Line, Wong Nei Chong Gap, Repulse Bay Hotel, St. Stephen's College and half a dozen other spots mentioned in diaries and official records. I took the funicular to the Peak and made my way along the boardwalk to the Mount Davis side, where I could look out over Aberdeen, the reservoir, the floating city of junks and the vast expanse of the South China Sea. The hillside was covered in spiky grass, small bushes and delicate wildflowers of the orchid variety. I stumbled on a cave large enough to hold a man. The hole in the ground seemed a perfect correlative to the depression I was in, so I spent several hours there thinking about the meaning of loyalty in times of war and peace and trying to imagine the feelings of soldiers, beleaguered and outnumbered here, so far from home and the familiar. All I got for my troubles was a chill. On the way down, I found a heavy chunk of metal about twelve by twenty-four inches, with rust forming around three shell-holes. Some blue paint still clung to the slab. Foolishly, I left it to the weather. I brought home, instead, articles from the *Hong Kong News*, ironic pieces making light of the Japanese victory and propaganda designed to win over the Chinese to the idea of A Greater Asian Co-Prosperity Sphere. No easy task for the butchers of Nanking. My co-tenants at the Chungking Mansions turned out to be call-girls, working for an escort service in Kowloon that catered to visiting businessmen. Margaret, the English one, told me she preferred Japanese men. Her other clients were wracked with guilt and constantly argued about the price; not so, the Japanese. They had class, treated the girls to dinner, wine, sometimes an evening out. Tradition, she explained to me. Yes, I knew something about Japanese tradition, especially Bushido. I maintained a casual, worldly air, but was really quite shocked by such goings-on. Jim laughed when I brought the subject up and made some joke about hotel rooms for the poor with wall-to-wall pussy. In Saigon, we called it keeping the world free for democracy, he said, while his Adam's apple moved under the laddered scar like a grenade. That night I drank too much and puked in the alley between Chungking Mansions and the Holiday Inn. And I dreamed of Margaret and others and their semi-precious gems.

DONNELLY

The real heroes of Hong Kong
were the cooks and comedians.

When we returned
half of us were impotent.
One vet committed suicide
two weeks after his marriage.
Porteous took 3000 milligrams
of niacine daily until he died.

All we ever talked about was food.
--Howard, did I ever tell you
about my mother's pecan pies?
--No, Jack, I don't think you ever did.
Of course it was the hundredth time.
After the war, Jack sent me
a bushel of pecans from Texas.

We kept recipe books
instead of girlie magazines.
We'd have traded *Playboy*
for *Betty Crocker*
any day.

MERRITT

Bastards stripped me of rank
for complaining of officers stealing food.
When I threatened to take it
to Brigadier Price of the Rifles
I got my stripes back quick.

What did we eat? We ate rats,
though they weren't plentiful,
a daschund, runaway pigs
from a Jap lorry, garbage,
a Labrador retriever. Maybe

you'd scrounge crabs along the shore
at the steel works. Sometimes
we'd steal rice from the Japs
and cook it a little at a time
in the soup pot, wrapped in a sock.

I'd have eaten one of them, too,
given half a chance.

FERGUSON

I used to dream
of pork chops

and I saw Major McCauley's arm
blown off.

I went down from 170 to 90 pounds;
no-one from back home,
not even the family,
recognized me.

O ya, and it cost 20 cents
to reach the barracks by rickshaw
after a Wallace Berry film.

Hell, I remember more
about the Halifax explosion.

LA FORTUNE

Rien à manger,
Rien à dire.

10

"What's this?" The prime minister scans
a 32-page letter attacking the *Duff Report*.
"George Drew must be crazy. Or underemployed.
Obviously, it's a cover-up;
you can't win elections,
or wars, for that matter,
with egg on your face.
He could spare me disclaimers
about not wanting scapegoats;
of course he wants them,
he wants the government
to fall into his lap.
Those poor devils who never tossed
a live grenade in training.
I'd have delivered them personally,
if they'd put one under you, George.
Spare me your lectures
on the nature and complexity
of the three-inch mortar;
and don't go on about Ralston,
water-carriers, McNaughton,
theatres of war. Homework, yes,
I'll give you credit for that.
But you're a bit sophomoric
in your displays of information.
Information ain't facts.
What do you know about 'evil influences'
at work in our midst, George?
I agree, Lyman Duff lacks subtlety.

He's too easily satisfied.
'Without a fighting chance'
—Hong Kong in a nutshell.
I envy you that one, George.
There's a bit of the old poet
in you, if a Conservative one.
Your hockey analogy was not bad,
either:

> It would be just as reasonable to suggest
> that men could be called trained hockey
> players who had been shown a hockey-stick, a
> puck and a goal-post and had their use
> explained to them, as it would be to say
> that men who had received lectures on
> weapons had actually been trained in the
> use of those weapons.

Not just Canadian content, George,
but a New Testament ring, to boot.
We could have used a man like you
on our side."

11

I don't suppose this information will be useful to you in your research, but I still have in my possession a letter written by my son, Private Andy Appleton, about three days after his arrival in Hong Kong. Apparently, he was on exercises in the New Territories—that's the section the Chinese want back in 1997—when he noticed the soil there was the same rust-red as here in Charlottetown, from all the iron deposits. He says he's putting a few grains in the envelope, but I guess the censors dumped it out when they cut out the names of several small villages. Maybe they thought someone would do a soil analysis and give away our positions. Anyway, Andy described various exotic flowers and plants in detail, including some sort of philodendron with huge, broad leaves the shape of tractor seats, the metal kind with sections cut out for ventilation or, perhaps, just to save steel. The picture he drew of the plant looked more like a skull, or one of those death's-head masks you see nowadays on goalies in the NHL.

Andy wouldn't have ended up dead in Hong Kong if I hadn't encouraged him to spend a summer in the Eastern Townships as an apprentice-surveyor for Lands & Forests. He met Paulette the same day he enlisted. She was working in one of those mobile chip-waggons near the armouries. Her father didn't approve of the war—he was some sort of nationalist—but he paid for the wedding and secretly wished Andy luck on his travels, toasting a victory from a small mickey of rye he kept on the rafters in the woodshed.

Andy may have been the first Canadian killed in action during World War II, but all he ever wanted to do was study plants. He was the kind of person who noticed things, correspondences. I'd like to think he got that from me. Paulette used to write to me during the war, but afterwards we lost touch. I knew what she looked like, though, from a snapshot Andy'd sent me. Then on June 12, 1951, ten years to the day after he'd enlisted and met her, she showed up on my doorstep with three small kids, all hungry and French as the day was long.

The photograph hardly did her justice, even ten years later. She was like a rare tropical flower, an orchid perhaps. She'd brought me one of his notebooks from the summer of surveying, with lists, descriptions and rather crude drawings, plus an old grey toque I'd knitted myself. She also showed me a letter she'd received from Hong Kong. It referred to that same afternoon in the New Territories. Paulette did not censor the tender passages, for which I was grateful; and, for my part, I never mentioned that I knew about plants with leaves the shape of tractor seats. We just sat there bawling and hugging each other, while the kids finished off another plate of scones and ran out to play in the red soil.

BERRIGAN

I'd been a teacher outside Yorkton,
So they put me in charge of the library.
There wasn't much variety,
so some guys had read the same book
a dozen times. After a while
they began to notice the words.

Four titles come to mind
as having more than literary significance
for our situation. One was Maugham's
Of Human Bondage, a sort of case-book
for the physically and mentally lame POW.
Then there was *Down the Garden Path*.
Someone had crossed out the author's name
and written in Mackenzie King.

Cheating Death was certainly popular,
but nothing had so much appeal
as Seton's *Wild Animals I Have Known*.
The text was surrounded with marginalia,
every blank space crammed with expletives
and commentary like biblical exegesis.
Seton was a Canadian and his stories
seemed to transport our captive audience
back home, even the stories set
in Nebraska and New Mexico.
I knew *Billy the Dog that Made Good*
and *Cute Coyote and Other Stories*
from my courses at teacher's college

in Saskatoon, but the all-time favourite
was "Lobo, King of Currumpaw," which describes
the capture and death of a wolf
after the killing of his mate, Blanca.
In the margin was scribbled: "Bullshit,
animals can't die of a broken heart."
Beneath that, in a very precise script:
"Don't be too sure, mate. Signed,
a fellow-animal."

I often wondered about Seton's association
with the Boy Scouts of America.
He accused them of being militaristic
so they threw him out in 1915,
ostensibly for not being an American.

PORTEOUS

I consoled myself
with thoughts of my wife
and lines of poetry
I'd memorized at school.

The silence of Ajax
is more eloquent
than words.

That helped me pass the night
in a drainage ditch,
watching tracers and fumes
from the hit refinery.
Then the waiting
and privations
made almost bearable
by concerts
I helped organize
in my official capacity
as YMCA officer.

Our fortunes lie
on the razor's edge,
O men of Iona;
Submit to hardships,
you will have to toil
for the moment,
but you will overcome
your fear.

Those are the words
of Dionysus in Herodotus.
While thoughts of her
kept me alive, my wife
had passed silently
into the dark.

250-WORD ESSAY REQUIRED BY THE JAPANESE ON THE BATTLE OF HONG KONG

On the southeastern shore of Lake Winnipeg, there's a small town called Libau. There wasn't much happening in those days to keep a town going, so we had to settle for a store, a garage and a barber-shop. The Japanese who took over the store in 1935 tried to sell sandwiches and coffee on the side and take in laundry, but nobody had money to pay for groceries, never mind the luxuries. After school, when my chores were done, I sometimes did odd jobs for Mr. Saeto in exchange for food. I piled wood, stocked shelves, or maybe brought him a catch of goldeye from the lake. The first time, I gutted them and cut off the heads and tails, but Saeto shook his head and made clear he wanted his fish intact. Kids used to say the Japanese ate fish-eyes as a delicacy, but I think Saeto used the head and tail for soup. He told me he had a wife in Japan and that he had been to visit her twice, the first time producing a son, the second time a daughter. I had a lot of respect for him when I heard that. Once, while we were warming our hands in front of the wood-heater, I asked him why he didn't bring his family to Canada. He told me politics was no good; it made people's hearts like stone. In all that time, I never even heard of Hong Kong.

249 words.

BORZOV

Optic neuritis or retro-bulbar atrophy:
blindness by any other name.
It set in after the first draft of Canadians
to Japan.

        They were trying to raise
a freighter just off shore; the stern
emerged, but sank twenty minutes later.

I'd started sketching from my perch
near the barbed wire, but found
I could no longer gauge depth
or draw a straight line.

        The gaunt faces
of my friends seemed more distorted
than usual in the cold December air.

Several of those on work drafts were lined up
for inspection, wearing sun-glasses
they'd made out of wire and broken bottles.
The cock-eyed lenses and skinny bodies
gave them the look of pumpkins on sticks.
I remember them fading as if a curtain
had been pulled over my eyes.
I just sat there in the sunlight,
brushes in my hand, thinking about Malory
and what he'd said to me after tenko.
You could hear the eerie notes of a Chinese flute
over the water.

Listen, he said, can't you hear it?
What? I said. Him, Delisle, still singing.
It's all that keeps me going, the knowledge
he won't stop singing.

12

From the offices of the *South China Morning Post*, I could watch the shipping in the harbour. Freighters of every size and registry lay at anchor, waiting to unload raw materials and pick up manufactured goods, much of it produced aboard the flotilla of junks that scooted like water-beetles over the skin of the bay. On the nearest of these junks, I could make out children going about their tasks. They were unschooled but sea-wise, tending animals, small shipboard gardens, running errands and, when they were not baby-sitting, helping at the sewing-machines and assembling gadgets or toys for foreign kids who hadn't dirtied their hands with anything but play. Floating factories that never stopped, despite the rotation of the earth and the invention of the calendar.

Still, there was a freedom of sorts. These descendants of traders and pirates, scorned and criticized for their unsavoury aspect and links with crime, were the secret envy of many underpaid and unprotected workers, who slept in shifts in the overcrowded slum-rises. They had helped Proulx escape and now many of them were running illegals from Vietnam, Cambodia and Mainland. For all I knew, the junk I could see refusing to give way to the Star Ferry and sending it off course might be harbouring some precious human cargo, stowed away amongst barrels of fuel oil and bales of cotton.

I'd have to tie things up soon. I had responsibilities to assume back home in Edmonton. I'd left a note on my office door that said, simply: GONE FISH-ING, IN HONG KONG. A lot of weight hung on that comma. And there was the matter of some articles I'd threatened to write for a friend at the *Journal:* Britain's expiring lease on Hong Kong; the current state of refugee camps; the night life and the black market.

"Why go to Hong Kong? You can get all the information you need from the computer data-bank and imagine the rest." We were sitting in the revolving restaurant of the Chateau Lacombe, across from his offices, while Edmonton disappeared under its annual snowfall. Two cars could not make the grade and were wedged, crosswise, on the road below. Everything was grinding to a halt. Me, too.

"I've got to get out of here. You're probably right about the book, but there are things I have to find out. Facts, you know, impressions. I've been writing journalism for so long, I've forgotten how to invent."

The waitress brought the refills we'd ordered and a bill. My friend was a regular, but never had more than two drinks, which he referred to as his lube-job. In a high powered business that produced as much stress as information, he was a bastion of health and good sense. He'd been a good eighth man, a key, on the rugby team too. He was turning the drink in his hands, and watching the amber liquid and ice gather momentum. When he stopped the glass, its contents continued their circuit of the container.

The junk had passed out of sight now, behind a high-rise under construction, one of those 35-storey human beehives that were replacing the 15-storey variety. Construction workers moved soundlessly on bare feet along the narrow planks and bamboo scaffolding, secured only with hemp.

BARDAL

You must be kidding,
we were heading the wrong way
up Corrigon Street.

Ya, ya, John Norris was beaten
by the Kamloops Kid.

You sure that thing's working?

I was an undertaker in Winnipeg
even before I joined up,
with all the jokes and cheap shots
the trade elicits. They stopped,
though, when the dying began.

Nobody wanted the photographs
and Hong Kong memorabilia
I'd collected over the years
and stored in a back room
with shoe-boxes full of unclaimed ashes.

You've got to push both buttons,
the PLAY and the RECORD.

Prison camp had its good points,
at least you knew what to expect.
When liberation came,
they had to pry me loose.
Back home, I felt stifled and resentful

and fled to New York
to lose myself in crowds.

I carried dysentery for six months
and memories I couldn't bury.

INOUYE

They used to call me the Kamloops Kid
and talk behind my back in camp.
I was born beside an orchard
in the Interior and went to school
in the Valley, beautifully cultivated
in terms of land, but not people.
I couldn't wait to leave and pursue
a civilized education in Japan.
They assumed I was just getting even
for the abuse I took as a kid
in BC, dodging the stones and insults
in the streets, being laughed at
and called a little yellow bastard
by the white gangs at harvest time.
After dark, I used to lob culls
into their midst around the campfire
like grenades and run like hell.
Actually, I got the shit kicked out of me
more often in the Japanese army
than at the hands of racists in Canada.
What finally broke my restraint was news
of the Evacuation, my mother and sister
in boxcars, like cattle, shunted
back and forth from Vancouver
to internment camps in the Interior.
I couldn't forgive those oversized bastards
for proving I was right, after all.
When I claimed immunity at the trials
in Tokyo, as a British subject.

the judged obliged by hanging me
in Hong Kong, Everyone
thought it a great
joke. Bad apple,
he said.

BATTEN

What's race got to do with it?
I was born in Liverpool
but came to Canada when I was two.

I started out on the Vickers
500 rounds per minute.
Damn good gun, but a bit heavy.
Takes three men, one on the gun,
one on the tripod, all three
carrying boxes of ammunition.

I remember instructing a platoon
of Poles not long after I joined up
in '34—I was with the Pats.
By the time I finished with those guys,
they could assemble by touch in the dark.

Then we switched to the lighter Brens,
with 50 rounds per minute in the clip.

I made it through the fighting,
the camps, even the coal mines in Oyama;
Then, coming home, the plane
hit an air-pocket over Honolulu
while I was in the can
and I broke my collar-bone
and three ribs.

13

Margaret asked me over breakfast if I'd store a suit-case for her in my room. She and her room-mate were in trouble with the Tongs for freelancing with clients and withholding money from the escort agency. They both expected a raid on the hotel, by the police or the underworld—it didn't matter which. I made some excuse about the possibility of a last-minute flight to Tokyo and not wanting to take responsibility for the stuff. Margaret smiled and said nothing further on the subject. I checked into the YMCA and made plans for a side trip to Lantau Island, two hours by boat from Hong Kong.

I wanted a sense of how things might have looked almost 40 years ago, when C-Force disembarked. It was raining on Lantau and the dirt roads were im-passable, so I sat in a hovel eating soup and rice gruel and watching a Chinese martial-arts classic in black and white. I might as well have stayed at the Y.

Back at the dock, the rain had let up. I looked around at the assembled passengers. Several tiny grandmothers, bearing huge bundles, were tending one or more small children; a couple of teenagers in blue terylene slacks were tearing at strips of fat-fried bread, stoking up for a night in the sweat-shops of Kowloon. Rubbish from Hong Kong nudged the pilings.

I was preoccupied with thoughts of the dangers Margaret was in and busy indulging in a little guilt for being such a shit, so I did not notice the apparition in Batman cape and mediaeval scholar's hat, the floppy velvet kind with a narrow brim running the entire circumference, who must have preceded me aboard. As the terminal slipped astern, this bearded emanation confronted me, a thin, white arm emerging from beneath the cape to present a business card and receive mine. I mumbled an apology for not having one and introduced myself.

KARL A. B. HELMSTRAND scanned me with cold, blue eyes and a hawkish intensity. His card was replete with graphics and Chinese calligraphy, spelled out for the uninitiated: KARMA, DEVA, TASHI. And there was an address on Lantau Island. After a few perfunctory questions designed to size me up, the obligatory lecture began. If I wanted to know about Hong Kong and the war, I should learn about the Overstately Powers (here, a thick, white eyebrow rose one inch), particularly the Jews, who had started the war and were behind every international incident.

Much as I tried to concentrate on Helmstrand's lecture, I couldn't help thinking about Margaret and the trip we'd taken the previous day to one of the refugee camps on Kowloon-side, not far from Kai Tak Airport. Inside the high metal fence and barbed wire, we were met by officials, quickly briefed and given over to the care of two refugee kids, a girl about eleven who took Margaret off for a tour of the dormitories and a one-armed boy in Hawaiian shirt, the kind manufactured with the wrong floral designs in Korea. He could tell I was neither an adoptive parent nor someone from an agency, so he asked if I had any cigarettes or dope. I gave him the pack of Players I'd taken to carrying in Hong Kong as ice-breakers.

My unofficial ambassador was Vietnamese. His sister had been a prostitute and made a lot of money from the Americans, which she'd salted away for the end of the war. She planned to take Benno with her to California. Ten hours after the last helicopter dusted the roofs of Saigon, she was killed by the liberating troops, three of them raping her first and taking her wristwatch. Benno was denounced by school chums who wanted to ingratiate themselves with the victors; then, when he was spared, they tormented him and tried to force him to reveal the whereabouts of the money. He was cut up with a machete and left for dead. What saved him was a cotton head-band he'd been given by a drunk Marine his sister had brought home one night. He wrapped that around the bleeding stump and twisted it tight with a screwdriver before passing out. When he woke, he was on the boat, wedged between two old people he'd never seen before, his new "family." The screwdriver and blue headband were gone, replaced by a stained bandage covering the stump, which had been charred to prevent infection.

Margaret was crying when I met up with her at the gate. "I'd like to take them all home," she said, dabbing at her eyes with a soiled Kleenex, "if only I had enough money."

Helmstrand's lecture was winding down. In only two hours, the subject had shifted from Moscow Bolsheviks to Sanscrit and back to the Overstately Powers, a veritable history of civilization illustrating

Arian superiority, the fundamental religious and linguistic unity of all Asians and a Jewish conspiracy to control the world. As we stepped ashore in Victoria harbour, his parting shot was a lesson in etymology.

"Your name has nothing to do with a fish; it comes from the Old Norse *gedda,* one who runs amok into battle."

I never saw Helmstrand again, nor any of the others, but I thought about his remarks. This fascist Santa Clause was mad as a hatter, but he was right about one thing. There are no observers, official or unofficial, in this game.

BAKALUK

You could hear the rumble of the bomb
70 miles away.

The Americans dropped
bras and panties—
then food.

First things first.

One relief container crashed through a hut
killing a POW.

On the way back home
I saw two movies in the canteen:
Donald Duck and *Frankenstein*.

The ship was called
the USS *Glory*.

14

The cobalt was not working.

The doctor had explained its use when the treatments began. Something about concentrated energy of the sun, contained in molecules or atomic particles, being beamed at the deadly reproductive cells in her body.

"Think of it as a war. We bombard the enemy cells at a faster rate than they can reproduce or be replaced by new troops and we win the war."

He smiles at the aptness of his analogy, pats her arm and adjusts the cannon of the huge cobalt apparatus so it is aimed at some point in her lower abdomen. My womb, she thinks, this is no place for a fight to the finish.

She's read in the morning paper that a delegation of Hong Kong Veterans from BC is going to Ottawa to see the Minister of Veterans Affairs about the long-overdue disability pensions. One, a former boxer and athlete from Victoria, has gathered a dossier of documents on medical problems peculiar to veterans of the Pacific campaign.

Not all the men had come home from the war. Her own had joined up, after all, and gone to Halifax as a hull inspector. Handsome in his blue uniform, but a little funny and self-important. He survived, but the marriage didn't. A chief petty officer. Just so.

The youngest is in the waiting-room of the clinic, reading comics and eating a bag of liquorice. His brother will be on the way home from school to deliver the *Sun*. Ann has agreed to adopt them, it's all settled.

"Do you remember when we were young, Ann, and used to walk our babies together in Stanley Park and talk about our hopes and fears? I said if I died first I'd send you the smell of roses, so you'd know I was nearby."

She recalls the blunt stern of the *Awatea*, as it churned seaward beyond the span of the Lions Gate Bridge, and the number of following gulls. The band was still playing "Good Night, Irene."

15

The atomic blast, which ends one stage
of the ordeal, ushers in another,
rendering life, as we know it, and art

impossible. So the poet, dreaming an epic,
produces, Sir, a few meagre voices
and chance fragments, random particles

that don't so much cohere as co-exist,
naked, stripped of familiar defences, but not,
for all that, without meaning or rhyme.

Plucked from the sidelines of history
into the very thick, he battles
insurmountable odds, codes and signifiers

in hand, his characters skirmishing
from particularity toward myth,
and attains a little advantage, some elevation

above events, a knoll or redoubt, where,
for a moment, perhaps, he can take stock,
regroup and view his muddied countenance

in a helmet full of rainwater.
Nothing of the shape he dreamed survives,
yet what he is and has imagined

is all there, ragged, dressed in motley,
the patchwork quilt he'd left behind at home,
where every swatch of cloth

contains some precious chunk of memory
not recorded in official documents.
Forgive him, Sir. He has stared too long

at the rising sun, gone blind.
The helmet is a fiction, like so much else,
to free him from the barbs of time.

Afterword

Two competing impulses are often at work in me as I feel a poem coming on: the pull of story and the pull of song. Lyric and narrative. I struggle with these two strong urges because I believe their marriage is important and worth preserving and because the kind of historical work I'm mostly engaged in requires both the linguistic intensity of lyric poetry and the power, drive and expansiveness of narrative. Conrad once described this process as *rescue work*, "gathering the vanishing fragments of memory and giving them the permanence of art." And the ancient Buddhist scribe, whose writings were hidden away for centuries in a secret 'library cave' in Dunhuang, near the eastern edge of the Taklamakan desert in China where the routes of the Silk Road converge, must have experienced something similar when he advised writers to "Sing as if narrating; narrate as if singing." Both of these challenges are what I have tried to do in the four narratives finding a new life here in *The Ventriloquist*.

Letter of the Master of Horse, my first and most abbreviated narrative poem, grew out of a misguided and frustrated desire to become an actor when I was a graduate student. I went with my friend Jeremy Hole to audition for Pinter's *The Caretaker* and Beckett's *Waiting for Godot* at the University of Toronto's Modern Drama Group. Jeremy got a role and I was offered the chance to man the telephone for ticket reservations. I took this rejection with the iota of stoicism I'd managed to dredge up for the occasion and retreated to my attic flat on Brunswick Avenue to mope.

Rummaging through my small library, I noticed an old Geography 101 textbook from my undergraduate days in Vancouver called *Weather: A Guide to Phenomena and Forecasts*. On page 59, I had drawn a circle around the illustration of a Spanish galleon with a blindfolded horse leaping off the stern, under the caption Horse Latitudes. On the way to conquer the Americas, ships carrying cavalry and horses were sometimes becalmed for extended periods with no wind and a diminishing supply of fresh water, so the crew were obliged to jettison the thirst-crazed animals into the sea. I couldn't get this image out of my mind and spent part of that night and the next, when I was supposed to be tending the phone to sell tickets, writing madly, producing a number of hysterical fragments that looked as if they wanted to be a poem. There was power in the images, but they needed toning down and a consistent voice. I required a speaker so close to the actual events that he could barely talk about them. That's when I realized it had to be the master of horse, a young lad driven to the brink of madness himself by the loss of the horses and subsequent violence, composing an imaginary letter to his sister back home in Spain.

War & Other Measures represents a big leap in terms of length and ambition as I struggled to understand what might drive a man to kill himself or consider killing others in so-called peacetime. To do this, I needed a larger canvas. When Paul Joseph Chartier died in a washroom of the House of Commons on May 18, 1966 at 2:15 p.m., after the bomb he was carrying exploded, the media response was quite telling: several journalists called him deranged; one dismissed him as an American copycat, because Canadians don't commit deadly individual acts; another, unable to see beyond the washroom connection, played the Freudian card, laughing at Chartier as an inept terrorist and a peculiarly Canadian version of the 'not-so-beautiful loser.' No one thought to ask if his death could have been a deliberate suicide or speculated on the politics and systemic racism that might have driven a sensitive French-speaking individual in Canada to consider violence or self-destruction. Whatever truth this long poem might have lies not in the 'facts,' but rather in the psychology, which has been revealed over and over again in Canada, as one group of citizens after another has found itself ignored, abused and frustrated to the breaking point.

The Terracotta Army emerged from a different kind of weather and experience, this time a trip to China with six other Canadian writers: Alice Munro, Robert Kroetsch, Adele Wiseman, Patrick Lane, Suzanne Paradis and Geoff Hancock. As guests of the Chinese

Writers Association, we were given an enthusiastic welcome, taken to several cities and historic sites, and expected to give talks to our hosts with the help of interpreters. Adele was the shining light in our group, as she rummaged in her green garbage bag full of her mother's handmade rag replicas of human figures, which included a 'philandering Frenchman,' and telling the story of each ragdoll in great detail as it was passed from hand to hand around the room. In Xian, the ancient capital, we were among the earliest foreigners to witness the life-sized pottery warriors and horses of Qin Shihuang, the first emperor of China, that were being gradually unearthed in what appeared to be an enormous airplane hangar.

An astonishing sight—and site—torsos half removed, an arm protruding from a wall of clay, a head lying metres away waiting to be retrieved and put back in place. I could feel those individual warriors reaching out to me, wanting their voices to be heard. Back home, I began to think about that colossal undertaking—an artistic equivalent of the Great Wall—and assumed to include at least 8000 terracotta figures constructed as insurance for the imperial afterlife. At night, mid-winter, sitting in my converted chicken coop and horse barn in eastern Ontario, I felt one of those soldiers, a charioteer, trying to tell me his story, which included his relationship with the master potter, Lao Bi. Old Bi, a wise, irreverent, irascible and hard-drinking trickster figure, was determined to resist the pressures of conformity and to make each of his vast army of soldiers as unique and life-like as possible.

When the charioteer had finished with me and slipped back into the realm of silence, it seemed as if the whole terracotta army had got the message and was lined up outside my office-barn door waiting to be interviewed.

Someone would later coin the phrase "ventriloquism of history," referring, I suspect, to all those voices from the past that take you by the throat and demand their story be told. It seemed to describe perfectly my creative process as a poet.

Hong Kong Poems also attempts to marry story and song. It's a narrative poem with intensely lyrical sections that owe as much to the pressures of friendship as to the attractions of historical research. Doug Elias, from the Museum of Man and Nature in Winnipeg, used to visit me in Victoria once a year for a brief escape from frigid Manitoba winters, and we would talk all night while wrapping ourselves around various quantities of good single malt scotch. On this particular visit, he told me about the museum's collection of interviews with Hong Kong veterans and the sobering story of their deployment and defeat.

Two battalions that constituted "C Force," the Winnipeg Grenadiers and the Royal Rifles of Canada, 1975 in all, were sent on a wrong-headed and ill-fated mission to defend the Crown Colony of Hong Kong against the possibility (read *inevitability*) of a Japanese attack. They arrived in Hong Kong on November 16, 1941, poorly trained, lacking weapons practice and without their military transport. The Japanese began their invasion on December 8, following a devastatingly successful attack on Pearl Harbour.

Vastly outnumbered by well-equipped and war-hardened troops, the Grenadiers and Royal Rifles fought bravely, but didn't have a chance. The battle raged for seventeen days before Hong Kong surrendered on December 25, not exactly what its defenders had in mind for Christmas. What followed for the surviving Brits, Canadians, Rajputs and Hong Kong Volunteers, now prisoners of war, was three and a half years of torture, slave labour, starvation and disease. Many died in captivity.

These tragic stories of war and conquest demanded to be told, and as powerfully as possible. I had little choice but to comply. The effort was at times unsettling, even excruciating, but the research, writing and shaping provided me with a degree of equilibrium. At its best, poetry speaks to the wound in each of us, the part of us that is damaged, incomplete, and so often in ruins. Which is exactly what Dylan Thomas, a poet with as many problems as gifts, had in mind when he wrote: "Out of the inevitable conflict of images—inevitable because of the creative, destructive and contradictory nature of the motivating centre, the womb of war—I try to make that momentary peace which is the poem."

About the Author

Gary Geddes has written and edited more than fifty books of poetry, fiction, drama, non-fiction, criticism, translation and anthologies and has received more than a dozen national and international literary awards, including the National Magazine Gold Award, the Commonwealth Poetry Prize (Americas Region), the Lt.-Governor's Award for Literary Excellence and the Gabriela Mistral Prize from the Government of Chile, awarded simultaneously to Octavio Paz, Vaclav Havel, Ernesto Cardenal, Rafael Alberti, and Mario Benedetti.

He taught English and Creative Writing for many years at Concordia University and has served as writer-in-residence at universities and libraries in Edmonton, Ottawa, Vancouver, Nanaimo and New Westminster, as well as Visiting Writer at University of Missouri-St. Louis and Distinguished Professor of Canadian Culture at Western Washington University in Bellingham. He lectures and performs worldwide. His work has been translated into French, Spanish, Italian, Dutch, Portuguese and Chinese.

He lives on Thetis Island with his wife, the novelist Ann Eriksson.

Manufactured by Amazon.ca
Bolton, ON